ANYTHING CAN HAPPEN IN A COMIC STRIP: CENTENNIAL REFLECTIONS ON AN AMERICAN ART FORM

M. Thomas Inge

Ohio State University Libraries, University Press of Mississippi, and Randolph-Macon College

1995

ANYTHING--
CAN HAPPEN---
Copr. 1947 by United Feature Syndicate, Inc. Tm. Reg. U. S. Pat. Off.—All rights reserved
IN A--
-DEC-19
COMIC STRIP

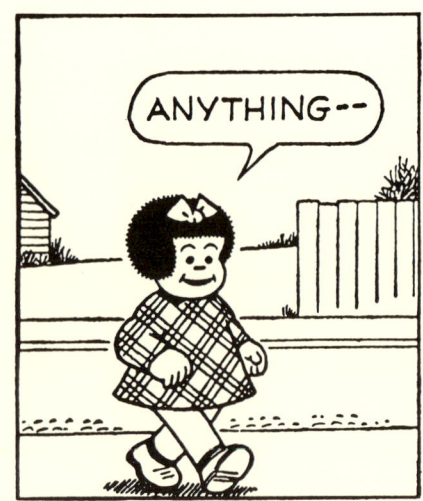

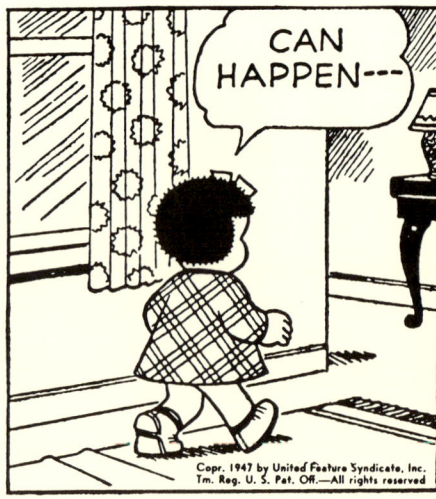

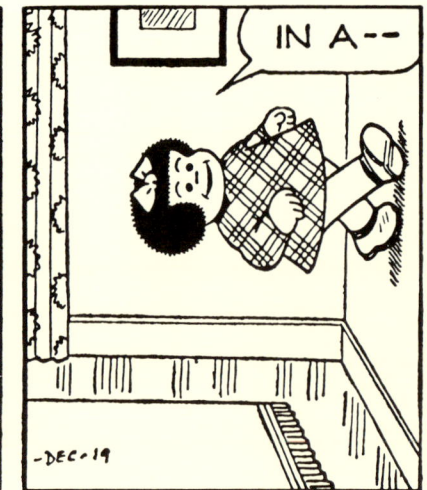

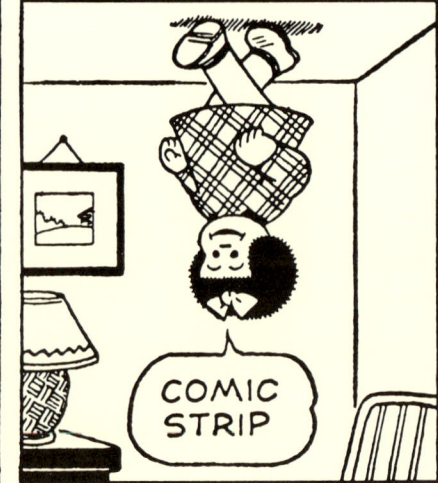

This catalogue is published as part of The Ohio State University Libraries' 1995 Festival of Cartoon Art to accompany an exhibition at the Columbus Recreation and Parks Department Cultural Arts Center 30 July-27 August, 1995. The Ohio State University Libraries, Friends of the Libraries, College of the Arts, and School of Journalism are co-sponsors of the 1995 Festival of Cartoon Art.

The 1995 Festival of Carton Art is underwritten by Universal Press Syndicate and companies in honor of their twenty-fifth anniversary.

Anything Can Happen in a Comic Strip: Centennial Reflections on an American Art Form is co-curated by M. Thomas Inge and Lucy Shelton Caswell. We are grateful to Dr. Ladell Payne, president of Randolph-Macon College, for his support. In addition, we wish to thank David W. Sims of The Ohio State University Cartoon, Graphic, and Photographic Arts Research Library; Seetha A-Srinivasan of the University Press of Mississippi; and Jennifer Johnson and Jennifer Mormon of the Columbus Recreation and Parks Department Cultural Arts Center.

Cover illustration: **Elton Dorval**
All Your Favorite Comics
1991.
Reprinted by permission of the artist.

Frontispiece: **Ernie Bushmiller**
Nancy
19 December 1947.
Nancy reprinted by permission of United Feature Syndicate, Inc.

Graphic design by Frank Pauer.

ISBN 0-87805-847-8

CONTENTS

ANYTHING CAN HAPPEN IN A COMIC STRIP:

CENTENNIAL REFLECTIONS ON AN AMERICAN ART FORM

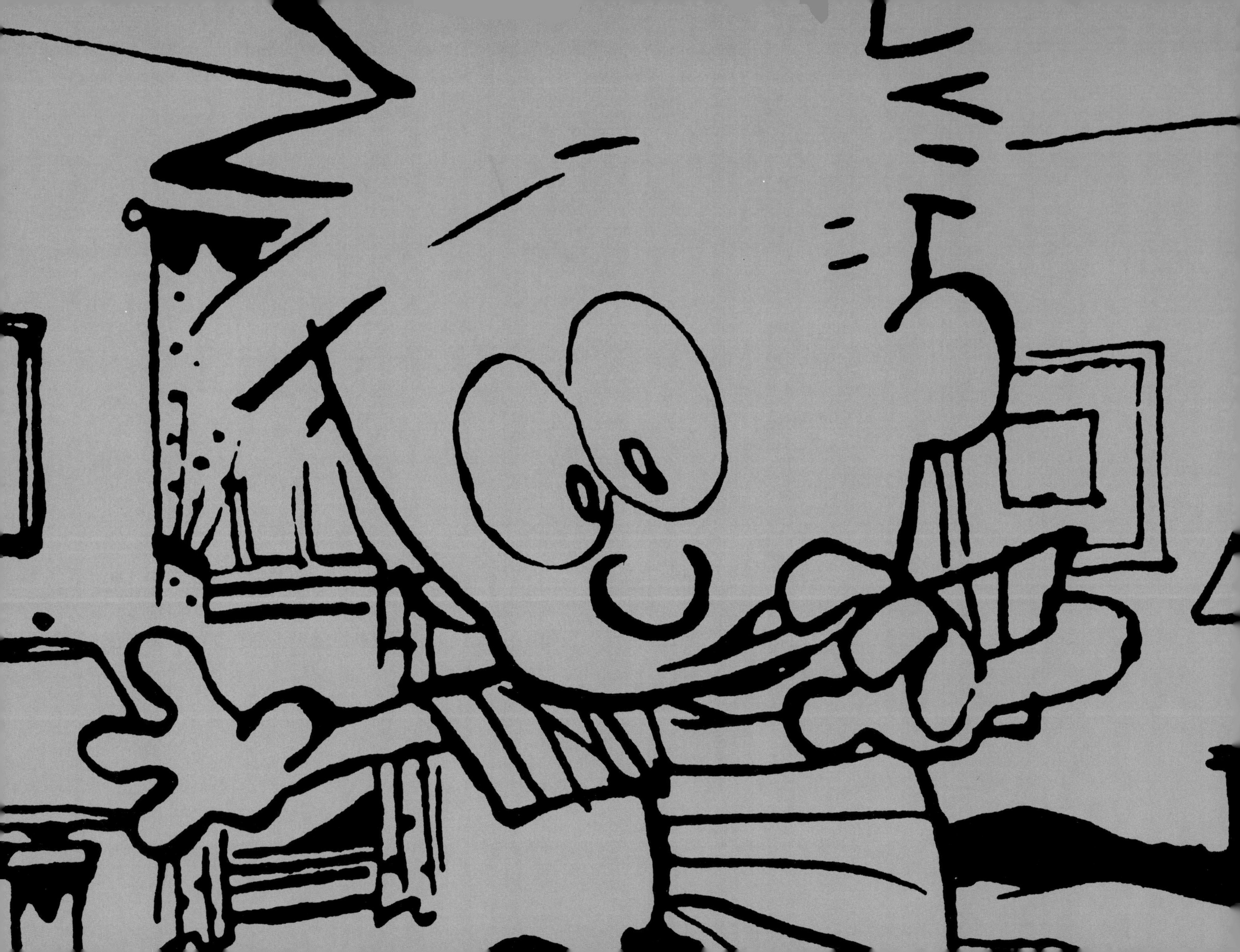

M. Thomas Inge

WANYTHING CAN HAPPEN IN A COMIC STRIP[1]

When Richard Felton Outcault introduced the Yellow Kid in 1895, the urchin was but one child in an alley heavily populated with a variety of ethnic children found in the urban ghettoes of New York City. The Yellow Kid both participated in the lively activities of Hogan's Alley and commented on the meaning of the action because Outcault brought the yellow-garmented kid into the foreground and had him speak directly to the reader by way of words scrawled on his shift. The Kid was a comic mediator occupying a middle distance between the other characters in the cartoon and the reader. Outcault's humor is enriched because we laugh at the children's antics, at the Yellow Kid's comments on them, and at the distance between our safe, orderly world and their chaotic, dangerous one. The cartoonist played on the complexity of his relationship with readers when on 20 September 1896, he had the Yellow Kid hold a letter from the artist apologizing to readers for being unable to answer his heavy fan mail and inviting a "pretty typewriter gal" to donate her services to assist him in catching up. Outcault's fictional mediator became a personal messenger as part of a playful scheme.

In 1902 Outcault began a comic strip about a character that became even more popular and lucrative: Buster Brown is an upscale mischief-maker, always properly dressed but constantly causing an uproar in his well-appointed home. Instead of using an article of clothing as a means of mediation and communication (as with the Yellow Kid), Buster employs posters to share with readers his resolutions to mend his behavior. Outcault seemed to need a dialogue between his leading character and readers. Interestingly, in a *Buster Brown* published in late 1903, Outcault was still seeking a "pretty typewriter," that is, a female typist, to help with his heavy correspondence.[2]

In 1907 Outcault brought the two worlds of his imagination together when Buster Brown, Mary Jane, and Tige visited Hogan's Alley and McFadden's Flats, both locations he used as residences for the Yellow Kid.[3] When the Yellow Kid meets Buster Brown, he comments, "There's another fellow who is being imitated like I was," a reference to the numerous imitations and plagiarisms of Outcault's successful characters. Outcault is using the Yellow Kid to voice his own complaint. After Tige and Buster are both attacked by the Kid's goat, Plato, Buster wakes up to find that the entire episode has been only a dream. The panel featuring Buster falling from his bed is a tribute to one of the most admired draftsmen in the history of comic art, Winsor McCay, and his beautifully drawn Sunday page *Little Nemo in Slumberland*.

Winsor McCay seldom broke the magic spell of Nemo's dream world with self-referentiality, but he did so in other features, especially the various dream strips he drew between 1904 and 1914. In a *Midsummer Day Dream* strip, McCay portrays himself at the drawing board unable to create because of intense summer heat.[4] After he dozes off, an idea comes in the form of a fuzzy, bird-like creature that escapes when the cartoonist working behind him interrupts to comment on the heat. In anger, McCay strikes the other man with his drawing board, only to discover he has been dreaming. This is, of course, an allegory about the elusive nature of creativity and how the slightest distraction can cause an artist to lose concentration.

Many would suggest that such comic strips are drawn when the cartoonist is totally out of ideas and can only dwell on him- or herself. Charles Schulz maintains that this is the lazy way out of a creative block.[5] There is, however, a long history and tradition of such sequences throughout the century newspaper comic strips have existed, and more often than not, as in the McCay dream strip, cartoonists turn the occasion into an opportunity to make a statement about the world of cartooning, its problems and limitations, or social and political issues.

Richard Felton Outcault *What They Did to the Dog-Catcher in Hogan's Alley.* 20 September 1896.

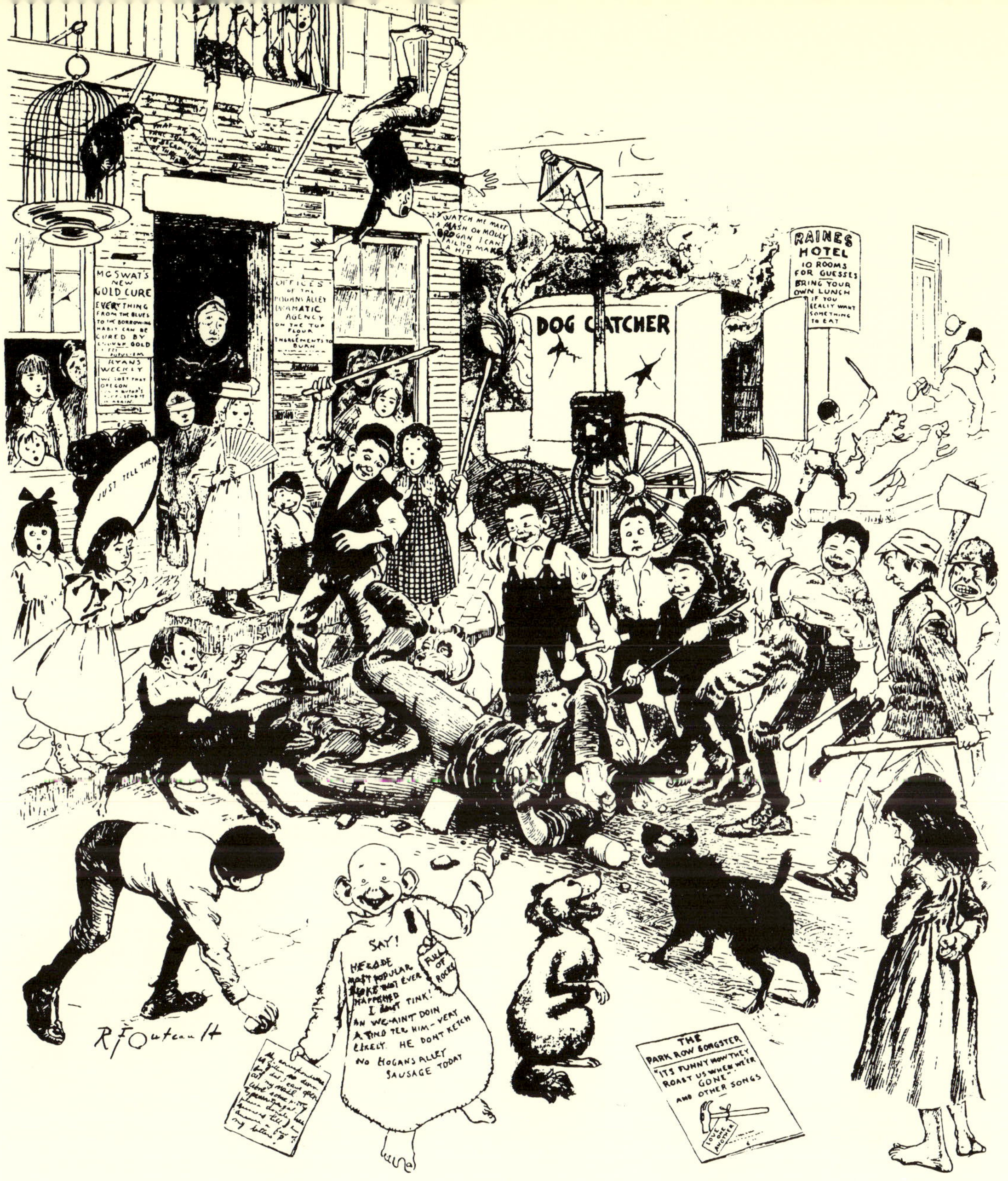
MC SWAT'S NEW GOLD CURE EVERYTHING FROM THE BLUES TO THE BORROWING HABIT CAN BE CURED BY
RYANS WEEKLY
OFFICES OF THE HOGANS ALLEY DRAMATIC AGENCY ON THE TOP FLOOR
WATCH ME MAKE A MASH ON MOLLY BROGAN I CANT FAIL TO MAKE A HIT
DOG CATCHER
RAINES HOTEL 10 ROOMS FOR GUESSES BRING YOUR OWN LUNCH IF YOU REALLY WANT SOMETHING TO EAT
JUST TELL THEM
SAY! HE'S DE MOST POPULAR BLOKE WOT EVER HAPPENED I DONT TINK! AN WE AINT DOIN A TING TER HIM - VERY LIKELY. HE DONT KETCH NO HOGANS ALLEY SAUSAGE TODAY
FULL OF ROCKS
THE PARK ROW SONGSTER "ITS FUNNY HOW THEY ROAST US WHEN WE'R GONE" AND OTHER SONGS
LOVE ONE ANOTHER
R F Outcault

WHAT THEY DID TO THE DOG-CATCHER IN HOGAN'S ALLEY.

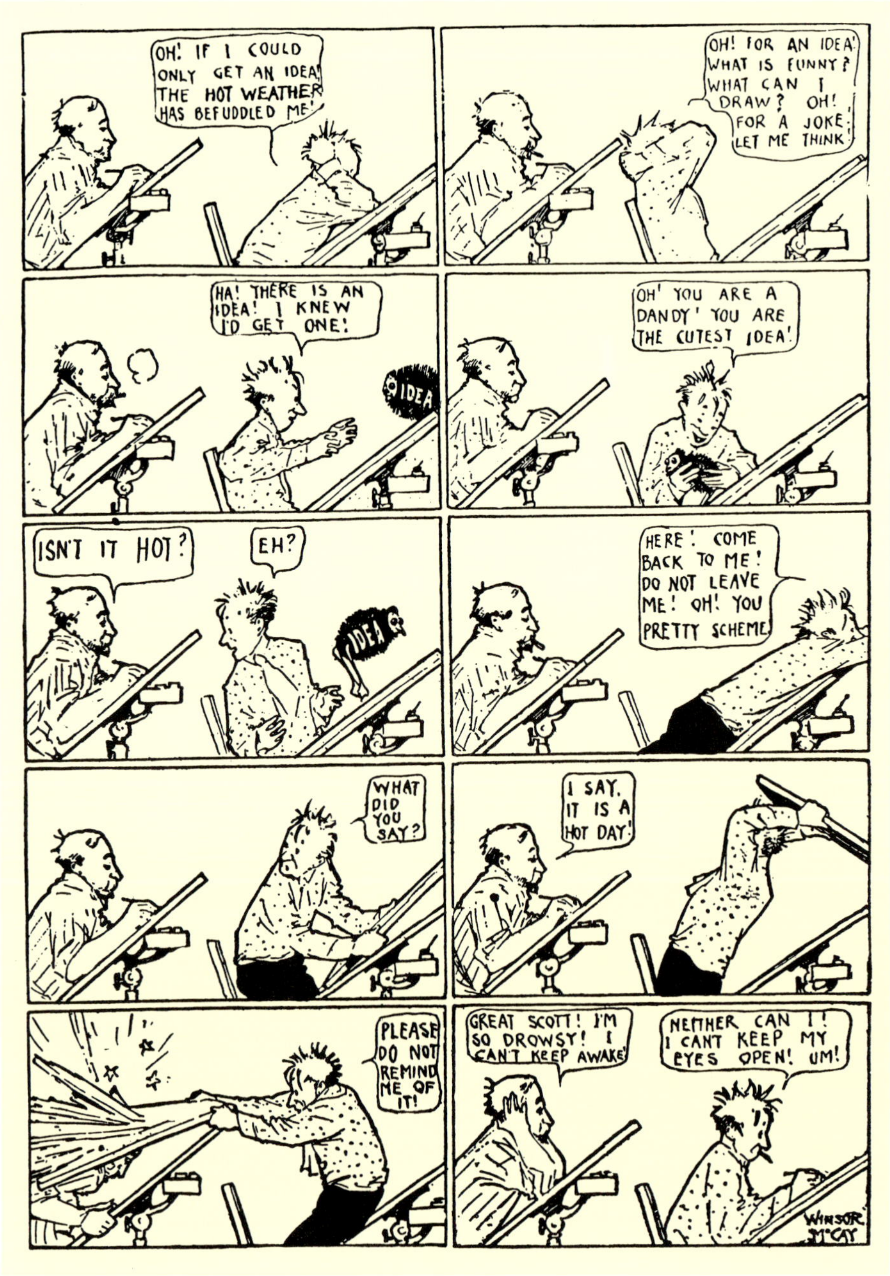
OH! IF I COULD ONLY GET AN IDEA! THE HOT WEATHER HAS BEFUDDLED ME!
OH! FOR AN IDEA! WHAT IS FUNNY? WHAT CAN I DRAW? OH! FOR A JOKE! LET ME THINK!
HA! THERE IS AN IDEA! I KNEW I'D GET ONE!
IDEA
OH! YOU ARE A DANDY! YOU ARE THE CUTEST IDEA!
ISN'T IT HOT?
EH?
IDEA
HERE! COME BACK TO ME! DO NOT LEAVE ME! OH! YOU PRETTY SCHEME!
WHAT DID YOU SAY?
I SAY, IT IS A HOT DAY!
PLEASE DO NOT REMIND ME OF IT!
GREAT SCOTT! I'M SO DROWSY! I CAN'T KEEP AWAKE!
NEITHER CAN I! I CAN'T KEEP MY EYES OPEN! UM!
WINSOR McCAY

Winsor McCay *Midsummer Day Dream*
ca. 1910.

In the 28 April 1919 episode of *Mutt and Jeff,* Bud Fisher portrays himself at the drawing board being berated first by the Republican and then by the Democratic newspapers for not doing enough to promote their causes, then by telegrams read by Mutt and Jeff dressed in army uniforms for supporting and not supporting the Bolsheviks in his cartoons, and finally by his editor who objects to his use of African American stereotypes. Little wonder that Fisher abandons himself to suicide in the last panel. He has experienced the job hazard of being unable to do anything that will please *all* of his comic strip constituencies. This is at least one of the reasons most comic strip cartoonists have avoided politics.

When George McManus reached artistic maturity and stylistic elegance in *Bringing Up Father* in the 1930s, he began to play with the technical conventions of the comic strip, breaking free of the limitations of sequential panels. In the striking Sunday page of 17 April 1938, an absent-minded character wanders by mistake into *Rosie's Beau,* the topper panel drawn by McManus to run above *Bringing Up Father.* When the man discovers his error, he simply climbs down into the first panel of *Bringing Up Father,* into the living room of Maggie and Jiggs. Apparently he has forgotten that he is to escort their daughter to a dance;

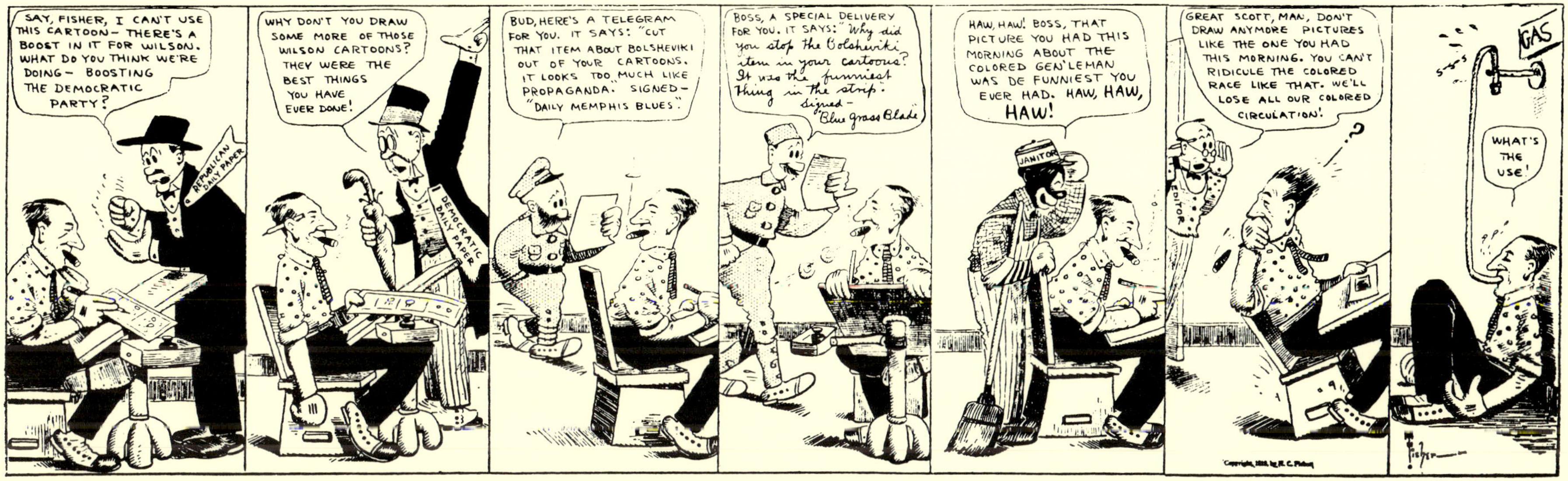
SAY, FISHER, I CAN'T USE THIS CARTOON— THERE'S A BOOST IN IT FOR WILSON. WHAT DO YOU THINK WE'RE DOING— BOOSTING THE DEMOCRATIC PARTY?
REPUBLICAN DAILY PAPER
WHY DON'T YOU DRAW SOME MORE OF THOSE WILSON CARTOONS? THEY WERE THE BEST THINGS YOU HAVE EVER DONE!
DEMOCRATIC DAILY PAPER
1919
BUD, HERE'S A TELEGRAM FOR YOU. IT SAYS: "CUT THAT ITEM ABOUT BOLSHEVIKI OUT OF YOUR CARTOONS. IT LOOKS TOO MUCH LIKE PROPAGANDA." SIGNED— "DAILY MEMPHIS BLUES."
BOSS, A SPECIAL DELIVERY FOR YOU. IT SAYS: "Why did you stop the Bolsheviki item in your cartoons? It was the funniest thing in the strip." Signed— "Blue grass Blade"
HAW, HAW! BOSS, THAT PICTURE YOU HAD THIS MORNING ABOUT THE COLORED GEN'LEMAN WAS DE FUNNIEST YOU EVER HAD. HAW, HAW, HAW!
JANITOR
GREAT SCOTT, MAN, DON'T DRAW ANYMORE PICTURES LIKE THE ONE YOU HAD THIS MORNING. YOU CAN'T RIDICULE THE COLORED RACE LIKE THAT. WE'LL LOSE ALL OUR COLORED CIRCULATION!
EDITOR
?
GAS
WHAT'S THE USE!

Bud Fisher *Mutt and Jeff*
28 April 1919.

but before he is reminded of this, he trips and nearly falls out of another panel and finally wanders into what he thinks is the library—only to find himself completely lost and out of the comic strip entirely.

On 2 January 1940, McManus began a practice which silently but effectively subverted any credibility in Jiggs and Maggie's world: a man in a picture hung on the wall leaned out of the frame in order to hear a nearby telephone conversation. Soon in most of the strips, figures in framed pictures on the wall began acting out their own miniature dramas and recreations, sometimes in counterpoint to the main action in the foreground.

The concept of creating self-reflexive activities in background pictures on the wall has a long history in illustration. For example, in one of Gustave Doré's illustrations for an 1867 edition of *Les Contes de Perrault*, a nanny is portrayed reading fairy tales to a group of children. Behind her on the wall is a preliminary sketch for another

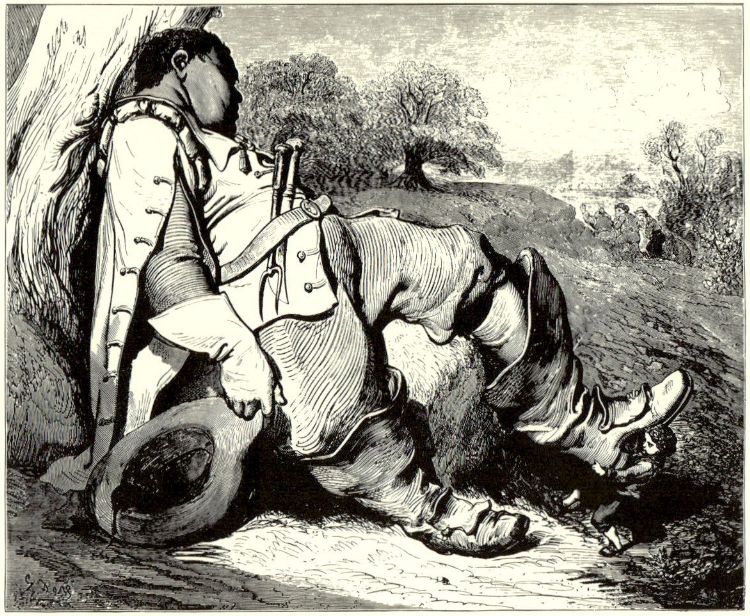

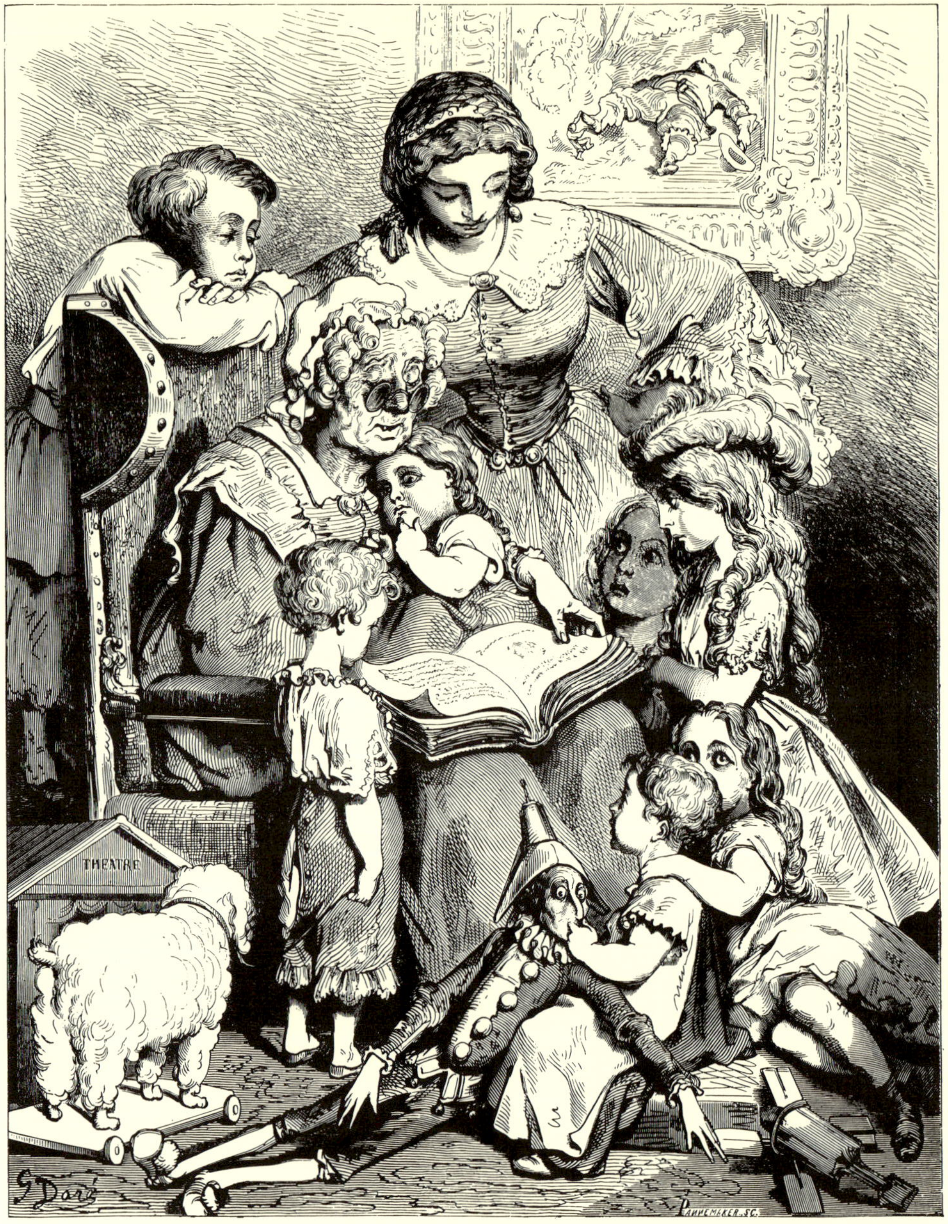
THEATRE

Gustave Doré two illustrations from an
1867 edition of *Les Contes de Perrault*
as reprinted on pages 113 and 117
of the 1967 Dover edition of
Perrault's Fairy Tales.

sketch by Doré found earlier in the same volume—Tom Thumb pulling the boots off an ogre—properly reversed in preparation for the engraver.[6] In Lewis Carroll's *Through the Looking Glass*, once Alice has passed through the mirror over the fireplace, she notices that "the pictures on the wall next to the fire seemed to be all alive, and the very clock on the chimney-piece . . . had got the face of a little old man, and grinned at her."[7] The original illustrator of the Alice books, John Tenniel, obligingly reflected this in his drawings, as did the American illustrator Peter Newell, even more vividly, in his 1902 edition.[8]

What has been called self-reflexivity or self-referentiality in art is a well-established tradition in fiction, poetry, drama, and painting. For instance, novelists such as Cervantes, Henry Fielding, Virginia Woolf, Jorgé Luis Borges, and Vladimir Nabokov produced works which self-consciously comment on the nature and conventions of fiction through revelations that suspend belief in the reality of the fictional world. These writers break the illusion of objectivity by speaking to us directly as author to reader, appear in their own stories as characters, parody other works and writers, and allow us a behind-the-scenes look at the process of creation. Such playful works have been called "metafiction" and

support the idea that all great fiction is primarily a reflection on itself rather than a reflection on reality. Whether or not that is the case, the device causes the reader to think about the relationship between artifice and reality. If art mirroring itself is a sign of sophistication and artistic control, an indication of an awareness of the limitations of a genre and the autonomy of the artist, it is interesting to note that in the comic strip, almost from the very beginning, cartoonists practiced self-referentiality and told readers that what they were reading was an artifice.

Metacomics may be divided into several categories. The largest is, perhaps, the crossover: the appearance of a character from one strip in another. Thus Tom Armstrong's Marvin looks into the mirror one day to discover that he looks like the cat Garfield. Another category includes those strips which pay tribute to or parody other comic strips by subtle reference or imitation of style, as when Bill Watterson did an entire sequence of *Calvin and Hobbes* (20-30 November 1990) in an admiring tribute to *Little Nemo in Slumberland* by Winsor McCay, the classic early strip mentioned above. A third category contains comic strips that use as a source of humor the technical conventions of the medium itself—the materials of production such as pencils, pens, ink, and paper; the

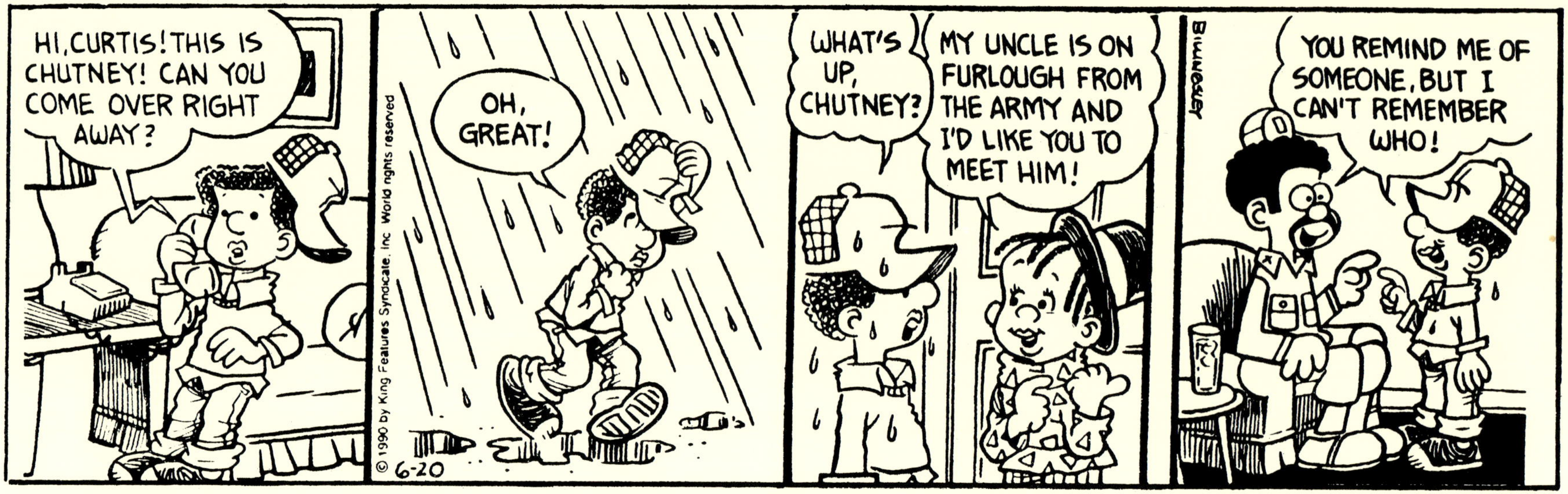
HI, CURTIS! THIS IS CHUTNEY! CAN YOU COME OVER RIGHT AWAY?
OH, GREAT!
© 1990 by King Features Syndicate, Inc. World rights reserved
6-20
WHAT'S UP, CHUTNEY?
MY UNCLE IS ON FURLOUGH FROM THE ARMY AND I'D LIKE YOU TO MEET HIM!
BILLINGSLEY
YOU REMIND ME OF SOMEONE, BUT I CAN'T REMEMBER WHO!

Ray Billingsley *Curtis*
20 June 1990.
Reprinted by special permission of King Features Syndicate.

borders or panels and the placement of dialogue within balloons; onomatopoeia and symbols suggesting sounds or emotion; and so forth: such comic strips explore the process of their own making. For instance, Bob Thaves on one occasion in *Frank & Ernest* even incorporated the copyright line into a joke (21 March 1989).

While metacomics have been part of the art of the comic strip from the beginning, in recent years their variety and frequency of appearance have increased. A sampling of comic strips collected between 1988 and the present fall into several categories as noted above. The crossover, perhaps the most popular type, is the comic strip version of what is known in movies and television as a guest appearance. Marvin discovers that his playmates at a new day care center are the infants from *Popeye, Family Circus, Snuffy Smith,* and *Hi and Lois* (5 December 1989). Camp Swampy's African American, Lt. Flapp, shows up for a visit in black-oriented *Curtis* by Ray Billingsley and proves to be Chutney's uncle (24 June 1990). Some crossovers indicate "real" connections, such as Beetle Bailey appearing in *Hi and Lois* (since Lois is Beetle's sister), most recently in several 1994 strips.

If a title or character is particularly popular, this, too, generates crossovers. Bill Watterson's *Calvin and Hobbes* has received numerous appreciative references in other strips, one of the more interesting being the day Calvin showed up with his stuffed tiger Hobbes to seek counseling from Lucy of *Peanuts*, but in a third strip—*On the Fastrack* by Bill Holbrook (10 September 1988).

What the crossover seems to suggest is that there is a comic strip world, a kind of Toon Town where the characters live together and get to know each other after hours. Since comic strips begin *in medias res* with an assumed history before we meet the characters and a continuing life after the story is over or the title ceases publication, the crossover supports the fact that comic strips are open-ended works without beginning or end, unlike most forms of narrative in Western culture. The artificial conventions of a beginning, a middle, and an end which pertain to most fiction do not apply to the comic strip.

A related category of metacomics contains strips referring to other comic strips, either explicitly or implicitly. Sometimes this is subtle, as when in the sequence of *Calvin and Hobbes* mentioned above, Bill Watterson demonstrated his respect for *Little Nemo in Slumberland* by Winsor McCay. Only those who know *Little Nemo*, where the central character would shrink or grow in size in accordance with the dream logic of Slumberland, are likely to catch the reference. When Berke Breathed was concluding *Bloom County* on 20-27 August 1989, his characters sought jobs in other comic strips: Oliver being bussed to *Family Circus*, Milo appearing in Gary Larson's *The Far Side*, and

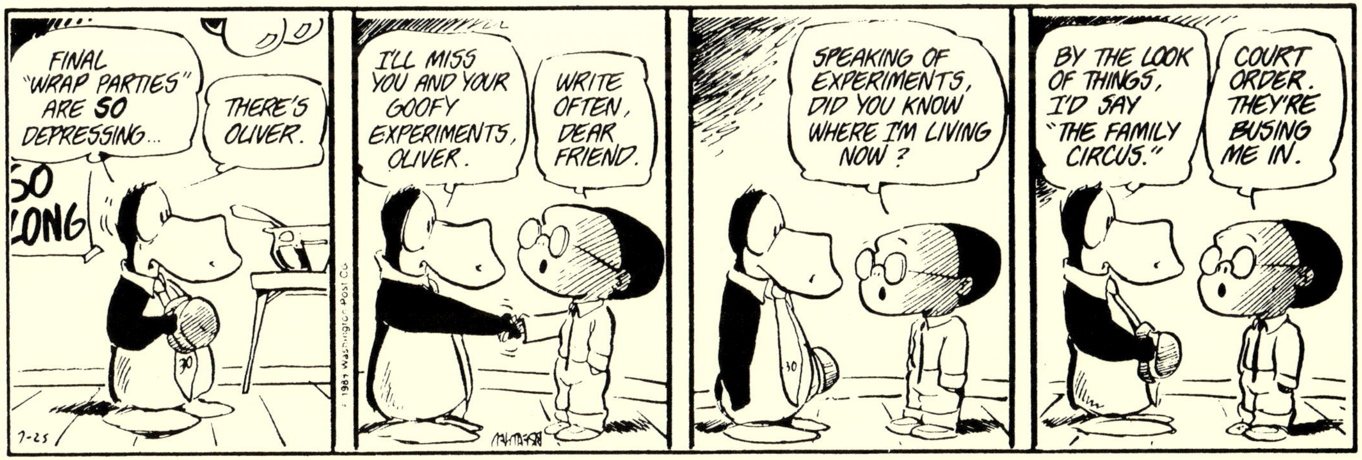
FINAL "WRAP PARTIES" ARE SO DEPRESSING...
THERE'S OLIVER.
SO LONG
I'LL MISS YOU AND YOUR GOOFY EXPERIMENTS, OLIVER.
WRITE OFTEN, DEAR FRIEND.
SPEAKING OF EXPERIMENTS, DID YOU KNOW WHERE I'M LIVING NOW ?
BY THE LOOK OF THINGS, I'D SAY "THE FAMILY CIRCUS."
COURT ORDER. THEY'RE BUSING ME IN.

Berke Breathed *Bloom County*
25 July 1989.
©1989, Washington Post Writers Group.
Reprinted with permission.

Portnoy and Hodge working as poop scoopers in Brad Anderson's dog panel *Marmaduke*. Steve Dallas first seeks employment in comic books, where the women are drawn large-bosomed and lusty, but he ends up trying to move in with Cathy Guisewite's single professional woman in *Cathy*, much to her dismay.

Most often, such references are simply designed to serve as a source of humor, as when Grimm begins to look like Popeye because Mother Goose is feeding him too much spinach (15 October 1990); but other functions are possible in crossovers. Both Garry Trudeau in *Doonesbury* and Berke Breathed in *Outland* have more than once courted a law suit from Walt Disney Studios by lampooning Disney characters and corporate attitudes towards ownership of those characters (see, for example, the 18 June 1990 *Doonesbury* and 19 November 1989 *Outland*). At least once a year in *Gasoline Alley*, Jim Scancarelli does a Sunday page paying tribute to some of the great comic strips of the past.

The third major category of metacomics is those which reflect on and use as a source of humor the technical conventions of the comic strip—the materials of production, such as pencils, pens, ink, and paper; the borders of panels and the placement of dialogue balloons;

the use of onomatopoeia and symbols to suggest sound and emotion; or the simplicity of language in the funnies. In one example from Johnny Hart's *B.C.*, a character asks where the world they inhabit comes from, and the other wonders if God invented India ink (25 June 1990). In a series by Garry Trudeau, Mike Doonesbury and other characters are caught in a week-long ink spill (12-17 June 1989) that causes them to talk back to their creator in rude ways. The reason for it, as we discover on the fourth day, was that Trudeau was simply without ideas that week.

Comic strip thought balloons have been satirized because of their obvious unreality in *B.C.* (25 October 1989) and *The Far Side* (2 April 1990). Berke Breathed devoted the entire 5 August 1987, Sunday page of *Bloom County* to the *Official Handbook for Better Comix Comprehension*, an overview of both real and invented terms for ways the comics can indicate emotions and expressions through signs and symbols. The inspiration behind this page may have been Mort Walker's satiric book on the conventions of comic art, *The Lexicon of Comicana*. The frequent comments on comics conventions in *Zippy* by Bill Griffith have included one about the simplicity of language that merges form with content (25 May 1990). On 19 August 1990, *The Far Side* panel

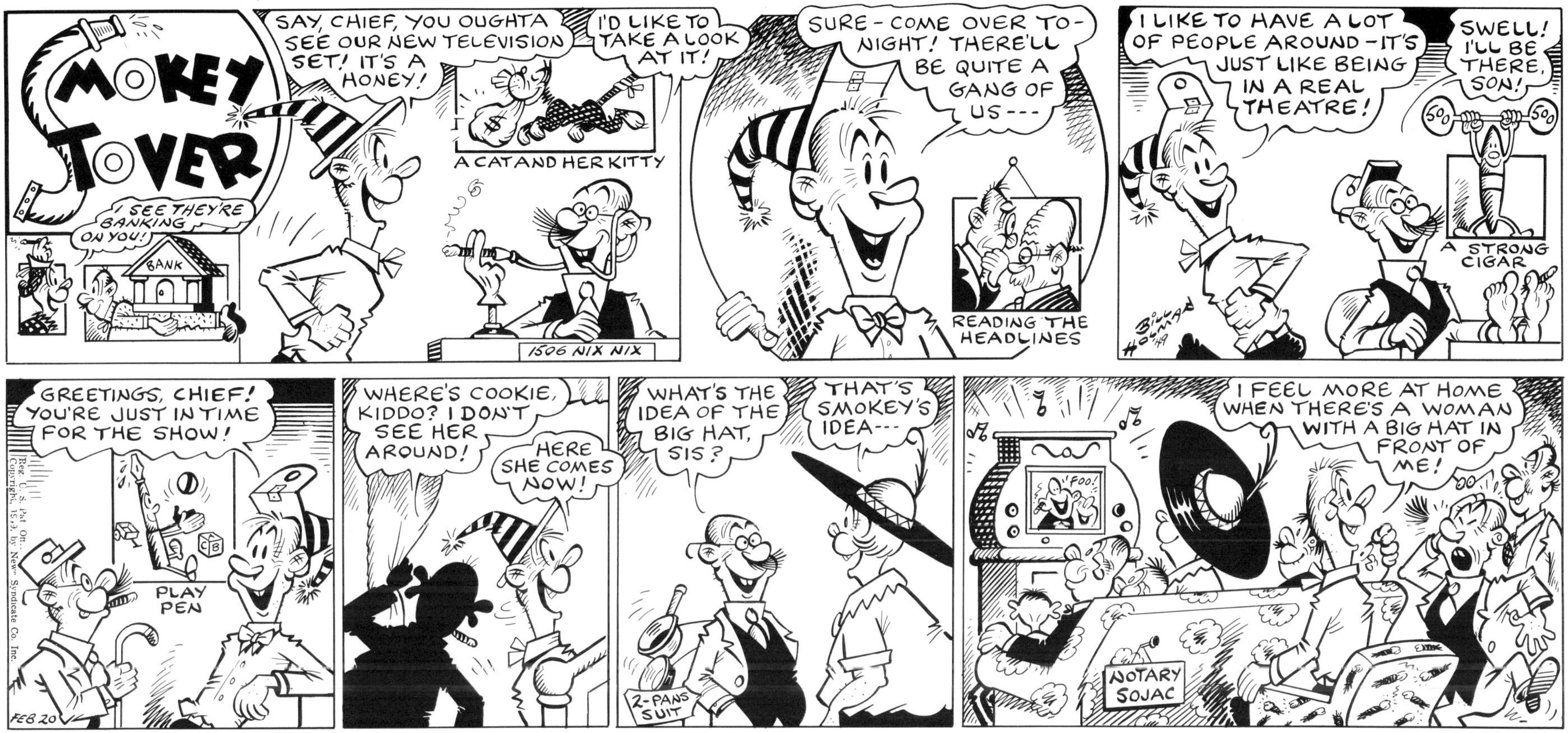
SMOKEY STOVER
I SEE THEY'RE BANKING ON YOU!
BANK
SAY, CHIEF, YOU OUGHTA SEE OUR NEW TELEVISION SET! IT'S A HONEY!
I'D LIKE TO TAKE A LOOK AT IT!
A CAT AND HER KITTY
1506 NIX NIX
SURE - COME OVER TO-NIGHT! THERE'LL BE QUITE A GANG OF US---
READING THE HEADLINES
I LIKE TO HAVE A LOT OF PEOPLE AROUND - IT'S JUST LIKE BEING IN A REAL THEATRE!
SWELL! I'LL BE THERE, SON!
500
500
A STRONG CIGAR
BILL HOLMAN '49
GREETINGS, CHIEF! YOU'RE JUST IN TIME FOR THE SHOW!
PLAY PEN
FEB 20
WHERE'S COOKIE, KIDDO? I DON'T SEE HER AROUND!
HERE SHE COMES NOW!
WHAT'S THE IDEA OF THE BIG HAT, SIS?
THAT'S SMOKEY'S IDEA---
2-PANS SUIT
I FEEL MORE AT HOME WHEN THERE'S A WOMAN WITH A BIG HAT IN FRONT OF ME!
FOO!
NOTARY SOJAC

Bill Holman *Smokey Stover*
20 February 1949.
Reprinted by permission:
Tribune Media Services.

reflects Gary Larson's obsession with morbidity and internal organs and pokes fun, as well, at the traditional idea that cartoonists should first master anatomy before turning to distortion and caricature. All of these examples, of course, decidedly puncture any notion of a sustained sense of realism in the comics and reflect on the general disposition among cartoonists to engage in self-parody of their profession and the artistic form in which they work.

The cartoonist who took self-referentiality to its most absurd limits was Bill Holman in *Smokey Stover*. Beginning in his Sunday pages for 1935, this wacky blend of slapstick and screwball comedy, visual anarchy, and verbal puns about a group of firemen resembled nothing so much as a colorful setting for a Marx Brothers film as conceived by Samuel Beckett. In the pictures on the walls, any number of hijinks are underway with a lively cast of characters, often with titles that are puns: A picture of a smoldering coat is labeled "Smoking Jacket";[9] or a drawing of two sets of women's panties—each appropriately colored—has the caption "Rose's are Red and Violet's are Blue."[10] Such vaudeville humor was often overlooked by the reader because of the other wild distractions taking place simultaneously on the page. *Smokey Stover* denied the laws of probability, gravity, and rationality in a comic strip which served to stretch the reader's willing suspension of disbelief. This was creative chaos in a postmodern mode.

The poetically whimsical *Krazy Kat* broke the conventions of its pen and ink world in inspired moments. On 25 January 1939, Herriman simply gave up inking the strip in the last panel, causing Offisa Pup to shout to the artist, "Wa-a-l . . . finish it!!! Y'got kartoonist's kramp?" The artist's procrastination prevents his characters from fulfilling their destiny, as outlined by the previous three panels which move from "transgression" to "apprehension" to "retribution": Ignatz the Mouse strikes his beloved Krazy with a brick and is jailed by Offisa Pup. In an intriguing Sunday page dated 1 June 1939, Ignatz draws himself engaged in his favorite sport of cat bashing in a cartoon within the strip. Since this is an imagined transgression rather than an actual one, the only retribution the representative of authority can enact is to start

his own cartoon of Ignatz in jail. While he is so engaged and distracted, Ignatz effects an actual violation of Krazy's complacent bean. In such metacomics, the line between fiction and reality becomes blurred. Since the world of the comic strip is already a fiction, what do we call the fiction within the fiction? Is it any less real than the fictional world of Krazy and what is the relationship of our world to it? Herriman raises these questions but leaves us to work them out on our own.

The cartoonist who may have provided the most complex development of self-referentiality in the comic strip was Al Capp. He began his hillbilly feature *Li'l Abner* on 20 August 1934, and for the first seven years he devoted himself solely to the characters and plot lines of the comic adventure strip that made him famous: A naive, patriotic, and singularly honest mountain boy, Abner Yokum, is continually pursued by an innocent, doggedly faithful, and extremely beautiful girl, Daisy Mae. Surrounding them was a family and backwoods community, Dogpatch, based on national stereotypes of Southern life and culture. But like the nineteenth century Southern literary humorists, Capp relied for his humor on exaggeration, dialect, the grotesque, and lively narrative action.

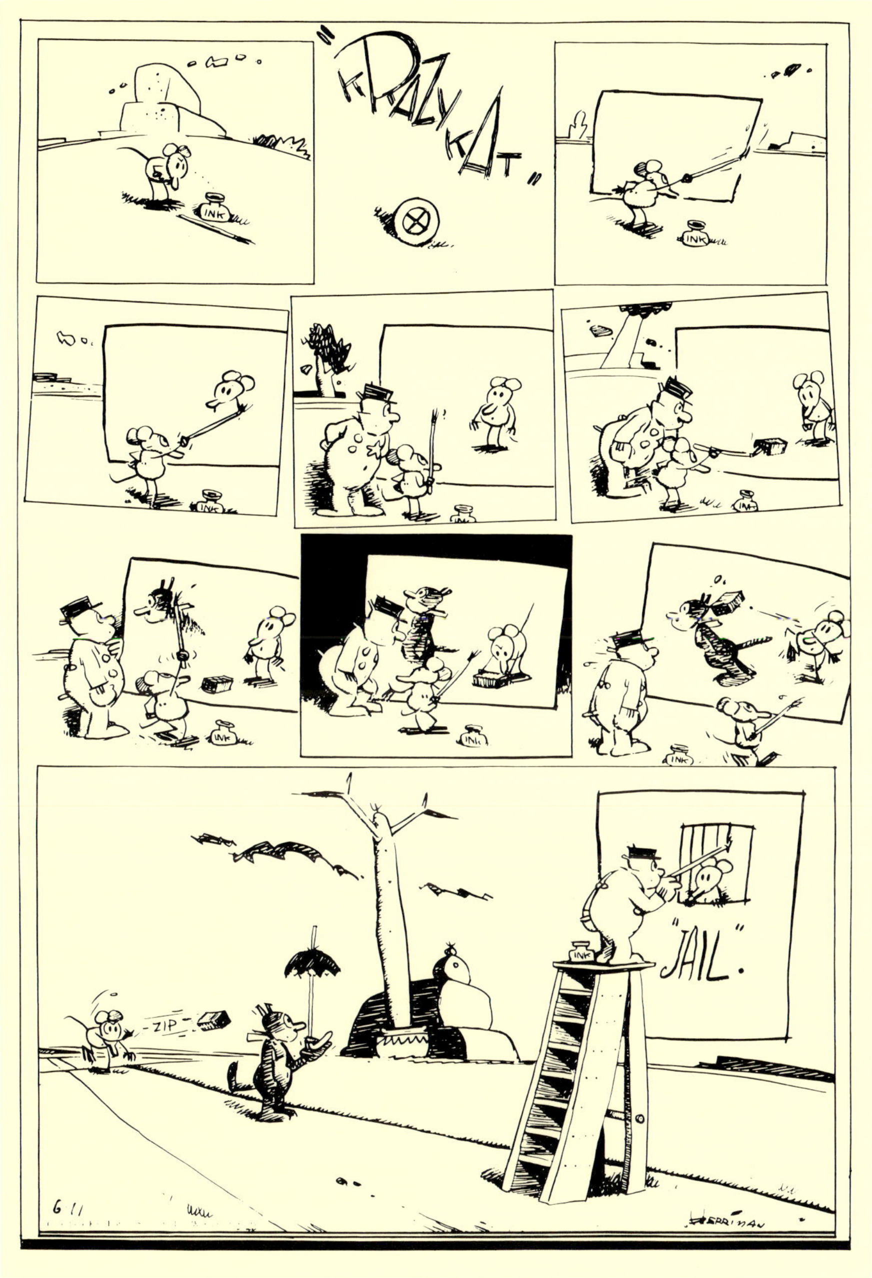
"KRAZY KAT"
INK
"JAIL"
ZIP
HERRIMAN

George Herriman *Krazy Kat*
11 June 1939.
Reprinted by special permission of
King Features Syndicate.

While Capp occasionally moved his characters to the big city for traditional comic encounters between country bumpkins and urban sophisticates, he did not disturb the insularity of the fictional world of Dogpatch until 2 June 1941, when he began a sequence about Li'l Abner's becoming a flying superhero. This was clearly a spoof on Jerry Siegel and Joe Shuster's character Superman, at that moment extremely popular in comic books, comic strips, animated films, and radio. It was the radio version that Capp's "Flying Avenger" was meant to satirize, and his newly discovered pleasure in the tool of satire soon led him to focus on other figures in the media: for example, on 6 January 1942, Capp introduced an Orson Welles look-alike named Orville Wolf, while Abner went in search of a girl named Cherry Blossom, a play on "Rosebud" of *Citizen Kane* fame.

Once Capp began to move his comic purview from straightforward character and plot to ironic commentary on other media, it was only a matter of time before he would ridicule his own strip. This he first did in a daily on 3 February 1942. Li'l Abner has presumably been killed by a bull in a Mexican ring, and he is laid out for the undertaker beneath the spread of an American newspaper. He awakens and leaves with the paper which contains a clue to his finding Cherry Blossom. The Mexican attendants return but are not as concerned to find Abner gone as that the newspaper is missing. "Ah well—the Americano was of no use since he was dad—but that newspaper had American fonnies een eet!" says one, and another replies, "Sigh! Now we weel nevaire know eef Senor Abnaire weel marry up weeth Senorita Daisy Mae!"

This was Capp's first step towards the concept of a comic strip within a comic strip, in this case, his own. *Li'l Abner* would never be the same, and a sign of things to come was an August 1942 Sunday page featuring a cartoonist named Lester Gooch who tries out on Abner a dangerous stunt to test its feasibility for use in his strip *Fearless Fosdick*.[11] Most readers understood this page and a subsequent one in November to be burlesques of the popular detective strip *Dick Tracy*, by Chester Gould, but there was no sign that these inside jokes would become a fully developed feature in Capp's strip.

Capp's own appearance in his strip came about involuntarily, because of a threatened lawsuit. In 1942 he read *Gone with the Wind*, which since its publication in 1936 and the release of the film in 1939, had become an infatuation of the American public. Capp began a parody called "Gone wif th' Wind" in a Sunday series

that featured Li'l Abner as "Wreck Butler" and Daisy Mae as "Scallop O'Hara." When the author, Margaret Mitchell, saw it, she was not pleased. Soon her husband, John Marsh, was on the phone with Capp and his syndicate threatening a multi-million dollar lawsuit if the series were not cancelled. They settled out of court, although the series ran for two more weeks because of advanced distribution to newspapers before it stopped in mid-sequence. Then in late December Capp drew himself into a Sunday page, using two panels to apologize to the people he sarcastically called "the Mitchells" rather than the Marshes, with Abner and Mammy Yokum insisting that he do so because "It's the Code of the Hills." Thus the social code of a fictional world was used to respond to the legal code of the real world as Capp momentarily stepped from the real world into his own comic strip's fictional world. By making himself a character at that point, the real Capp shielded himself from having to apologize personally, something he must have been loathe to do given the innocence and playful nature of the parody to begin with. Any other author than Mitchell would have been happy with the free publicity generated by a Capp lampoon.

Visits by the Yokums to Capp's studio and drawing board began in the daily comic strip series on 1 January

1945, when Abner dropped by to find out what fiendish adventures awaited him in the year ahead. At this point, Abner showed an awareness of himself as a comic strip character under the control of his creator and established the grounds for a dialogue between author and actor about the nature of the genre and its limitations. All of this Capp's readers accepted without losing their intense interest in Abner's escapades or their faith in the integrity of the comic strip world he inhabited.

The cartoonist's complex relationship with his readers had already been expanded in a sequence which began 16 June 1944, when Fearless Fosdick and his creator Lester Gooch were reintroduced for a longer story in the dailies. During the 1940s the top five comic strips, each appearing in over twenty-five million newspapers, were *Li'l Abner*, Chic Young's *Blondie*, Ham Fisher's *Joe Palooka*, Harold Gray's *Little Orphan Annie*, and Chester Gould's *Dick Tracy*, so Capp was taking on one of his main competitors, though reportedly with Gould's permission.[12]

Dick Tracy was known for its gothic atmosphere, brutal violence, and grotesque villains physically misshapen in ways reflective of their names—Pruneface, the Mole, B. O. Plenty, Gravel Gertie, and the Rhodent

among them. Gould's art was already an example of stylized caricature, so Capp had but to move the parody to a higher level of exaggeration: Bullets pass through hats and bodies leaving large holes, brains are blown out in neat circular wedges, eyes are gouged, and extreme torture is visited upon Fearless Fosdick's pliable body. Plot lines are carried to absurd extremes. For example, in a 1949 sequence "The Case of the Poisoned Beans," one can of baked beans out of the millions on store shelves has been poisoned by a diabolical villain. Fosdick sets out to protect the public from itself by simply shooting any citizen he sees preparing to eat a can of beans.

No matter how stupid his behavior, Fosdick remains Li'l Abner's hero, "th' ideel of all red-blooded American boys." Dick Tracy, too, retained his following despite his humorless demeanor and simple-minded devotion to police procedure, not to mention the unbelievable rescues from impossible circumstances of danger and imminent death. At first, Gould enjoyed Capp's parody, seeing it as a way of promoting *Dick Tracy*, but as Capp developed the feature and it created its own following, Gould reportedly became exasperated and stated "Enough's enough!"[13] But the complaint came too late.

Capp's Fearless Fosdick sequences proved over the

BY GEORGE, FOSDICK—YOU'LL ENJOY THIS NEW CASE! THE WORLD'S WORST CRIMINAL, AGAINST THE WORLD'S WORST--OOPS!--EXCUSE ME-GREATEST DETECTIVE!!
FRANKLY, I NEED A NEW CASE LIKE I NEED A HOLE IN THE HEAD!!
4-22
YOUR OPPONENT, FOSDICK, IS A MERCILESS KILLER WITH A FANTASTICALLY PLIABLE FACE!!—HE CAN PUSH IT INTO ANY SHAPE—AT WILL --INSTANTLY!!
HM-M! INTERESTING--
"ANY FACE," HE IS CALLED!!—YOUR ORDERS ARE TO GET HIM!! THE ONLY CLUE WE CAN GIVE YOU IS---
Cop. 1947 by United Feature Syndicate, Inc. Tm. Reg. U. S. Pat. Off.—All rights reserved
—HE MIGHT BE ANY BODY!!—
IT WILL BE NICE TO GET BACK INTO ACTION AGAIN, SIR. I CAN HARDLY WAIT—
Al Capp

Al Capp *Li'l Abner*
22 April 1947

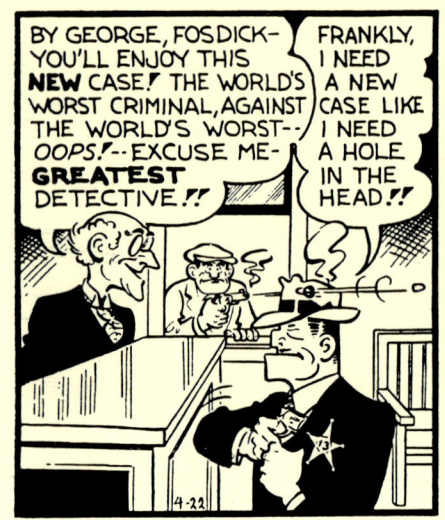

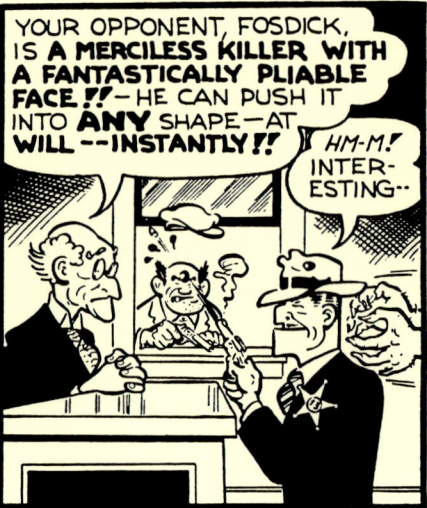

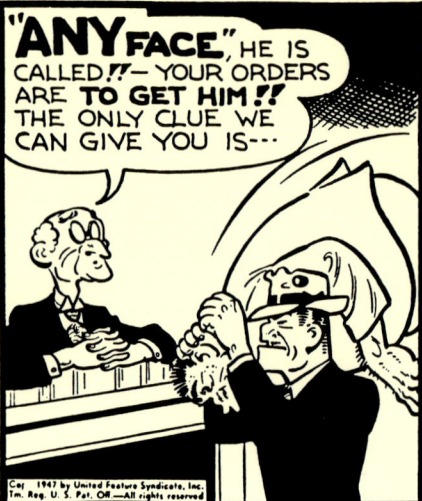

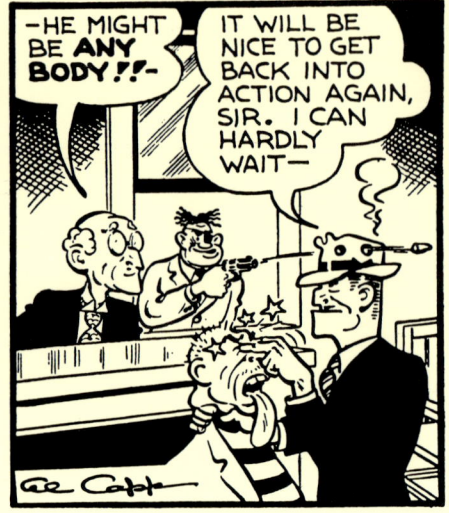

years to be some of his most popular. Several of the stories were reprinted in the *Li'l Abner* comic book series (and promptly became collector's items), several were published as a book in 1954, a television series was based on the feature using puppets the same year, and Capp used the character in a series of successful advertisements for Wildroot Cream Oil hair tonic. *Fearless Fosdick* remains the only comic strip within a comic strip to achieve its own following. Such title-specific referentiality is unusual in the comics, but the end result is to underline the fact that the internal conventions of the genre bear little relationship to the real world, although reading *Dick Tracy* may be a part of that world. In addition, both *Dick Tracy* and *Fearless Fosdick* served to puncture the realistic pretensions and actual romanticism of the popular gangster films of the Thirties and the *film noir* of the Forties, a kind of conversation with other media the comic strip has always conducted.

Capp used self-referentiality for a variety of purposes over the years—often for personal rather than artistic reasons—but self-referential parody reached its fullest complexity not in his hands but with the unwitting assistance of another talented cartoonist, Will Eisner, creator of his own crime fighter, the Spirit, who appeared weekly nationwide in a newspaper comic insert. As one of the most skilled artists and storytellers ever to practice comic art, Eisner had a strong coterie of readers and fans, Al Capp among them.

Capp had long felt that, like most cartoonists, he was underappreciated and underpaid by United Feature Syndicate. The best known example of corporate mistreatment of cartoonists is that of Jerry Siegel and Joe Shuster who sold their rights to Superman for a few hundred dollars to their publisher, who in turn earned billions of dollars from merchandising. When in 1947 they attempted legal action to share in the profits, they were fired from further work on their creation. Capp satirized the publisher's treatment of Siegel and Shuster in a 1947 Sunday *Li'l Abner* sequence about two starving artists who create *Jack Jawbreaker* (actually a detached muscular arm moved by a small propeller).[14] Their syndicate agent, Squeezeblood, sells the feature for $500 a week but passes on only $5 to the artists because he thinks money would spoil their creative genius.

Also in 1947, Capp filed suit against United Features in New York Federal District Court, alleging several breaches of contract, demanding $14,000,000 in damages, the cancellation of his current contract, and total ownership of the property *Li'l Abner*. Capp was a master in using other media to promote his comic strip. (Just a year before, as an adjunct to the story line, he had somehow persuaded six of the most popular radio personalities—Frank Sinatra, Kate Smith, Danny Kaye, Bob Hope, Fred Waring, and Jack Smith—to broadcast on their shows a song he had written for Daisy Mae to keep Abner from marrying another girl.)[15] To help his own case, Capp used false pretenses to persuade Will Eisner to help with his crusade against his syndicate. Capp telephoned Eisner and suggested that they start a print

feud in their respective features by satirizing each other's characters as a way of generating reader interest. Eisner was flattered by the attention of one of the nation's most popular cartoonists and began working on a story called "Li'l Adam, the Stupid Mountain Boy." (This story is reprinted in its entirety in the Appendix.)

Published 20 July 1947 in the Sunday *Spirit* supplement, the story opens in the studio of Al Slapp on a stormy night just as he has apparently been shot by an unseen assailant. The scene shifts to Commissioner Dolan's office where Mr. Matrix, manager of the Knight Feature Syndicate, is enjoining the police to check on Slapp, who has not answered his phone, because of his value to the syndicate for the 5,000 newspapers that purchase his *Li'l Adam* comic strip. In a speech by Matrix that compliments Slapp's intelligence and keen wit, Eisner cleverly works in references not only to the *Gone with the Wind* incident but also to Capp's parodies of *Dick Tracy* and Harold Gray's *Little Orphan Annie*:

> After he finished with "Off with the Breeze," the author Maggie Malone, never wrote a book again. You, of course remember how he took the popular *Nick Stacy* strip and by cunningly changing the name to *Fearful Fooznik* made its

cartoonist, Hector Ghoul, a laughing stock! And lately he seized upon that great sentimental comic, *Little Homeless Brenda*! . . . Brrr I feel sorry for Elmer Hay, its creator!

The Spirit, who has nonchalantly been trying to get out of the police station with his fishing gear, sarcastically comments, "A Voltaire of the comics, eh?" People like John Steinbeck and Charlie Chaplin had, in fact, been paying Capp such high-toned compliments.[16]

Unable to escape the assignment, the Spirit visits the other artists who might have had it in for Slapp, looking for clues: Elmer Hay, who looks just like Daddy Warbucks in *Little Orphan Annie* (including Gray's distinctive style of drawing round eyes without pupils, about which there is some wonderful byplay in the story), and Hector Ghoul, who looks more like Fearless Fosdick than Dick Tracy. While both provide cause for suspicion, Matrix is finally revealed as the culprit because Slapp was leaving him to sign with another syndicate. Then Slapp, having only been stunned, wakes up and leaves, only to be socked by a hillbilly with Li'l Abner's body and Pappy Yokum's head, for making hill people out to be so stupid in his strip.

Eisner got his entire staff to work on the story,

including having the young Jules Feiffer draw the *Dick Tracy/Fearless Fosdick* parodies so that the styles would differ. The story is filled with in-jokes and topical references—such as the circulation wars between syndicate moguls William Randolph Hearst (called Richard Headline Smirch) and Robert R. McCormick (Hobart D. McDornick), the creative tools of cartoonists, and their practice of returning favors by sending an original drawing (in the days before such an item became a collectible with a high market value).

Capp apparently tipped off *Newsweek* magazine about what Eisner was doing: Eisner found himself featured in a story a week before his story appeared in *The Spirit*, but in the context of Capp's lawsuit. Once Capp accomplished his goal, he never returned the favor by satirizing *The Spirit* in one of his *Fearless Fosdick* sequences. Eisner has stated:

He never did anything in his strip about *The Spirit*. I kept watching and waiting, and nothing happened. I then realized that he had euchered me into doing a parody of *Li'l Abner* which *Newsweek* picked up, and he had been given a run of publicity. I was simply being used as a tool.[17]

Nor did Capp send Eisner an original drawing.

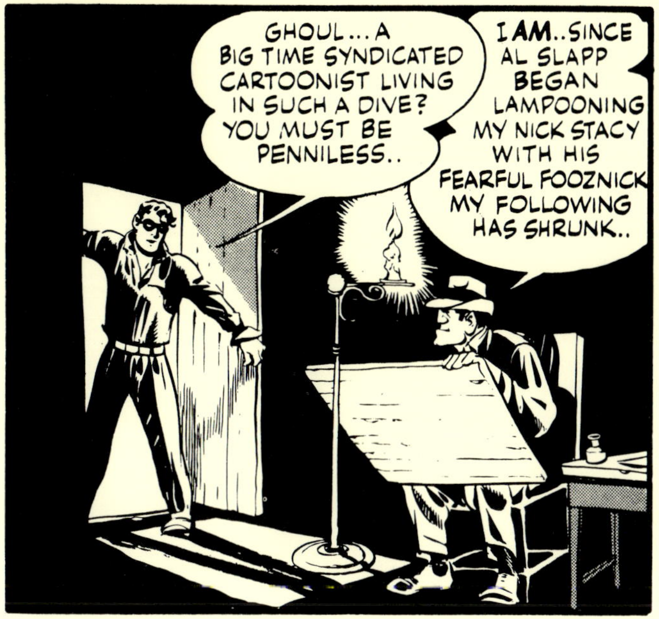
GHOUL... A BIG TIME SYNDICATED CARTOONIST LIVING IN SUCH A DIVE? YOU MUST BE PENNILESS..
I AM..SINCE AL SLAPP BEGAN LAMPOONING MY NICK STACY WITH HIS FEARFUL FOOZNICK MY FOLLOWING HAS SHRUNK..

Will Eisner "Li'l Adam, the Stupid Mountain Boy," *The Spirit*, 20 July 1947. (detail) ©1974 Will Eisner. Reprinted by permission.

Will Eisner never harbored a grudge against Capp, who treated most of his cartoonist friends in such a cavalier way; and *The Spirit* did receive influential publicity from the incident. What is more important, however, is the brilliant *tour de force* Eisner accomplished in this single story. It is at one and the same time a specific satire of Al Capp and *Li'l Abner*, a parody of Capp's parody of *Dick Tracy*, a parody of Harold Gray's *Little Orphan Annie* and its unabashed sentimentality, a comic critique of the business practices of syndicates, and a general satire of the entire profession of cartooning. No other strip in the history of American comic art has achieved such a multi-layered self-referentiality as this one, and it remains a singular feat: a metacomic without equal.

That the cartoonists' community noted the episode is indicated by the fact that a year later the entire incident was itself parodied by Harvey Kurtzman in one of his single-page comic book fillers *Hey Look!* published in the second issue of the Marvel title *Lana* in October 1948. A character walks sequentially through four panels reading the funny papers and noting Eisner's "take off" of Capp's "take off" of Gould, which is seen as a "take off" of Chic Young's *Blondie*, before the speaker finally "takes off" as an airplane. Kurtzman cleverly imitated the techniques of all four artists and the clothes of the narrator change according to each stylistic context.

During its best years of the 1940s and 1950s, Ernie Bushmiller's *Nancy* achieved a type of purity in its humor and minimalist art, and self-referentiality was part of his stock in trade. As Brian Walker has observed in *The Best of Ernie Bushmiller's Nancy*, ". . . he deliberately broke down all the barriers of time and space to entertain his readers. Distorting perspective, defying the laws of gravity, decapitating his characters—Bushmiller experimented with every possible combination of design and concept. . ."[18] Nancy walked onto the ceiling, commenting "Anything can happen in a comic strip" (19 December 1947). On another occasion she unsuccessfully tried to

IF YOU INSIST ON RUNNIN' OFF TO BE A ORPHAN GAL, YOU'LL GOTTA BE HAVIN' A CURLY WIG 'CORDIN' TO THIS FUNNY PAPER.
YEP.
THIS DOG IN HERE IS A DULL SORT OF CLOT-POLL ... COULDN'T WE BREAK THAT UP A LITTLE?.. I LIKE A LARGER VOCABULARY.
WHAT'S WRONG WITH "ARF?"
ALWAYS THOUGHT DOGS SAID "RALPH." WELL, WE COULD CALL YOU "HEY, NONNY NONNY."
THEM THERE CRITTURS GOT BLANK GLASSY EYE BALLS ... SEE KIN YOU LOOK LIKE THAT.
THEN WE CAN CALL THE TEAM "LI'L ARF AN' NONNY"....... ....MY WORD... IT'S DIFFICULT TO SEE THIS WAY, ISN'T IT?
IT EVIDENT DON'T MATTER MUCH.
9-11
DIST. BY POST-HALL SYNDICATE
COPR. 1952 WALT KELLY

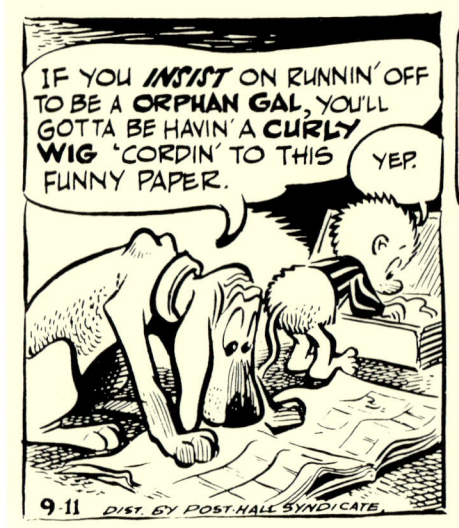

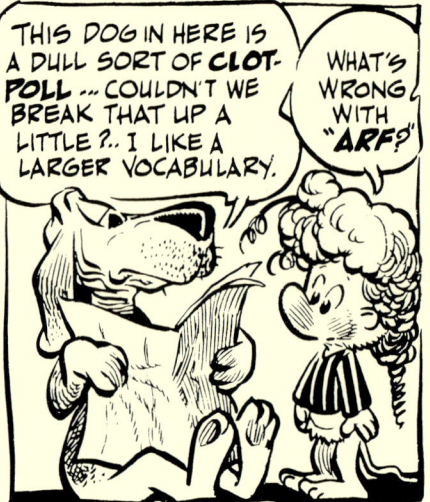

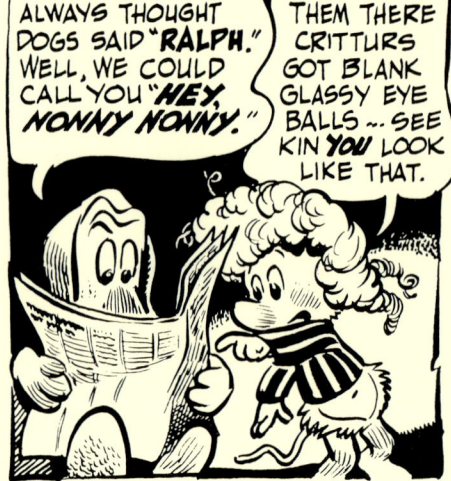

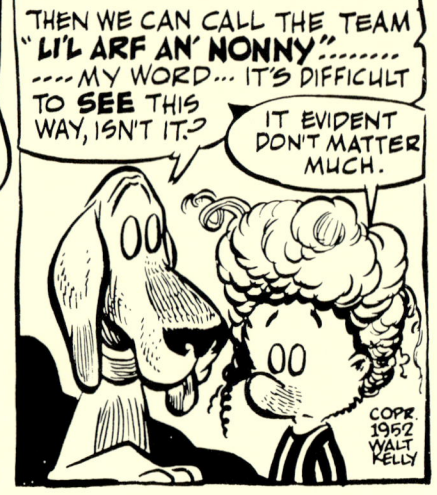

Walt Kelly *Pogo*
11 September 1952.

walk beyond the length of the panels to make her point that it is better to plan ahead (2 September 1958). "More so than any other cartoonist of his era," Walker notes, Bushmiller ". . . used himself as a character in his own strip. His drawing hand, grasping the flexible-nibbed cartoonist quill, frequently entered Nancy's world from stage right. Nancy and Sluggo referred to him as 'the boss' and worried about his condition when the lines weren't drawn just right."[19]

Although he claimed that his intention was always to "dumb it down,"[20] Bushmiller was clearly an artist of great skill and intelligence, who knew how to manipulate his comic strip in innovative and postmodern ways, while making it look simple. Because he made it appear so easy, *Nancy* was dismissed by many readers as one of the least funny strips on the newspaper page. If Pirandello deconstructed the modern stage on behalf of a drama reflective of the uncertainties of reality and the truths of fiction, Bushmiller did much the same thing for the comic strip. But the pessimism of Pirandello's worldview yields to Bushmiller's gentler and sweeter comic incongruity.

During its twenty-four-year run from 1949 to 1973, Walt Kelly's *Pogo* became America's favorite source of political satire under the guise of funny animals acting like human beings. Shaped by his experience in Disney's animation studios, plus drawing fairy tale and fantasy comic books for children, Kelly's style was both whimsical and acerbic through his use of body language and facial expression to capture human attitudes. While the *Pogo* characters had distinct personalities, they were easily molded into caricatures of the political stances of the

American public; and many a prominent figure found himself portrayed in the strip as some suitable animal bearing striking resemblance to the original person.

Since the entire intent of *Pogo* was to comment on reality (except in its purely whimsical moments), Kelly frequently felt no compunction about allowing the characters to discuss the nature of comic art and the pen-and-ink world they inhabited. Sometimes the humor was directed at other comic strips, such as the occasions when Pogo and Beauregard Hound would dress up as characters in Harold Gray's *Little Orphan Annie*. All Annie parodists enjoyed ridiculing Gray's style of drawing eyes without pupils, which in the case of Pogo led him to walk into trees or fall into streams. What is a useful convention for one cartoonist becomes absurd if placed in the context of another comic strip of different conventions.

In an elaborate Sunday page for 8 March 1964, Kelly stages a conversation between Albert and Pogo that constitutes an essay on Kelly's own drawing style (which Pogo compares unfavorably with that of the much-admired Milton Caniff), the possibilities and limitations of cartooning as a profession, and the ingredients of a successful comic strip feature, with glancing reference to the lack of faith modern young people have in the "old time icons" and traditions. Always prone not to take

Jerry Dumas and **Mort Walker** *Sam's Strip*
16 August 1962.
Reprinted by special permission of King Features Syndicate.

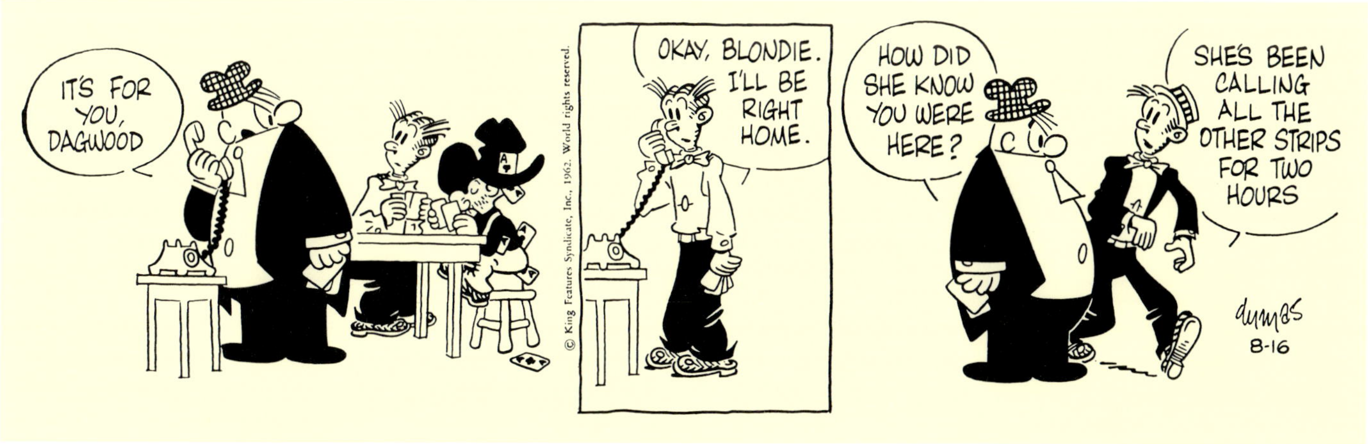

IT'S FOR YOU, DAGWOOD
© King Features Syndicate, Inc., 1962. World rights reserved.
OKAY, BLONDIE. I'LL BE RIGHT HOME.
HOW DID SHE KNOW YOU WERE HERE?
SHE'S BEEN CALLING ALL THE OTHER STRIPS FOR TWO HOURS
dumas
8-16

himself too seriously, Kelly even questions the underpinnings of his own successful feature when Albert says that when you cannot draw "You makes cartoon animals talk." Pogo responds, "Who'd believe in talkin' cartoon animals?"

Although it achieved only limited circulation and lasted less than two years between 1961 and 1963, *Sam's Strip* by Mort Walker and Jerry Dumas is the only strip entirely devoted to comic strip history. The lead character, Sam, occupies a world populated by characters of past and present comic strips. Snuffy Smith plays poker with Dagwood Bumstead; Sam tries to persuade Ignatz Mouse to stop throwing bricks at Krazy Kat; or some eighteen characters, ranging in age from the Yellow Kid and Happy Hooligan to Moon Mullins and Pogo, gather at the Comic Characters Convention.

The source of the strip's humor is nearly always some convention of the genre: emphatic use of language and onomatopoeia, physical exaggeration, stereotypes, and various artistic styles. Sam's is a self-referential world

Mort Walker *Beetle Bailey*
17 October 1994.
Reprinted by special permission of King Features Syndicate.

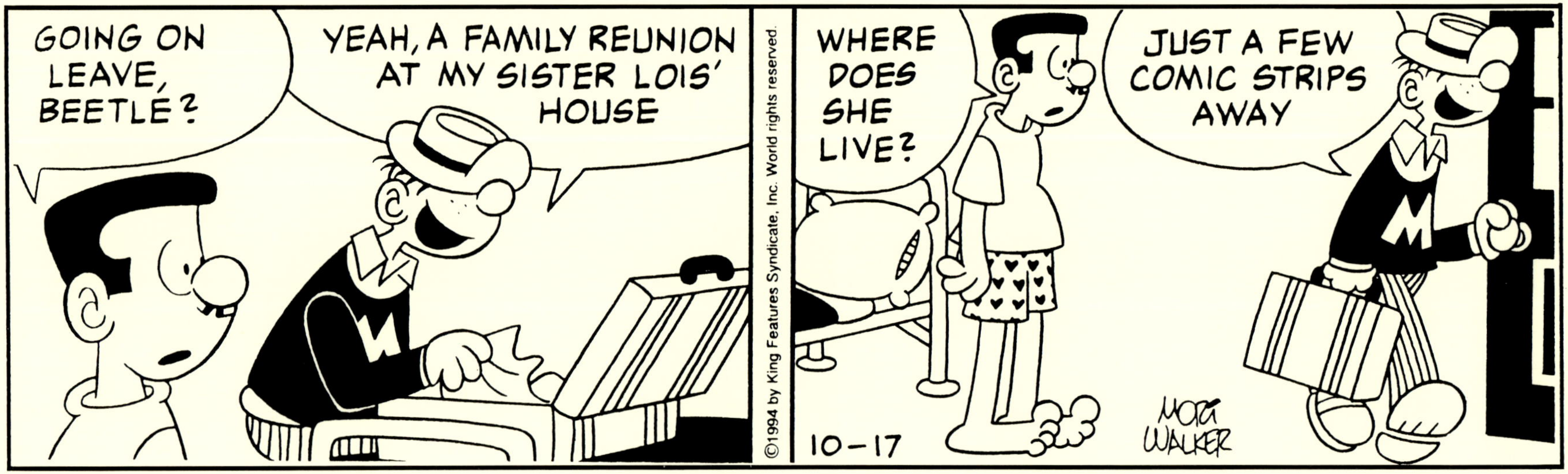
GOING ON LEAVE, BEETLE?
YEAH, A FAMILY REUNION AT MY SISTER LOIS' HOUSE
©1994 by King Features Syndicate, Inc. World rights reserved.
WHERE DOES SHE LIVE?
JUST A FEW COMIC STRIPS AWAY
10-17
MORT WALKER

where all of the characters live in a state of existential suspension. Readers with little knowledge of the history of comic art in all of its forms (editorial and gag cartoons, as well as comic strips) are not likely to understand many of the strips, which may have been one of the reasons for its short life. For those who know and love the comics, it is a treasure, and it may be the only pure metacomic we have had.

A comic strip which defies definition but plays with self-referentiality more often than not is Bill Griffith's *Zippy*, a product of the underground comix movement that crossed over into the mainstream newspaper comics pages. Under the name Griffy, the cartoonist is one of the strip's leading characters along with the titular figure, originally known as "Zippy the Pinhead," signifying his origin in the "pinheads" with pointed craniums which were once staples in carnival freak shows before public sensitivity to physical deformity closed them down. (Griffith borrowed his directly from Todd Browning's 1932 classic cult film *Freaks*.) The comic strip provides

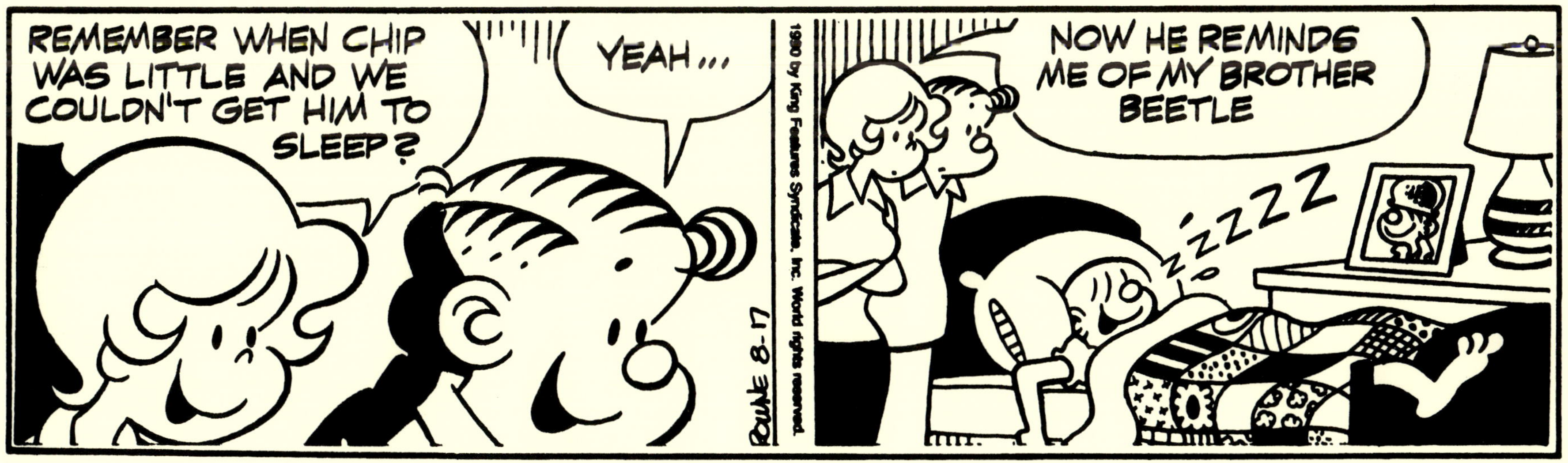
REMEMBER WHEN CHIP WAS LITTLE AND WE COULDN'T GET HIM TO SLEEP?
YEAH...
BROWNE 8-17
1990 by King Features Syndicate, Inc. World rights reserved.
NOW HE REMINDS ME OF MY BROTHER BEETLE
ZZZZZ

Mort Walker and **Dik Browne** *Hi and Lois*
17 August 1990.
Reprinted by special permission of King Features Syndicate.

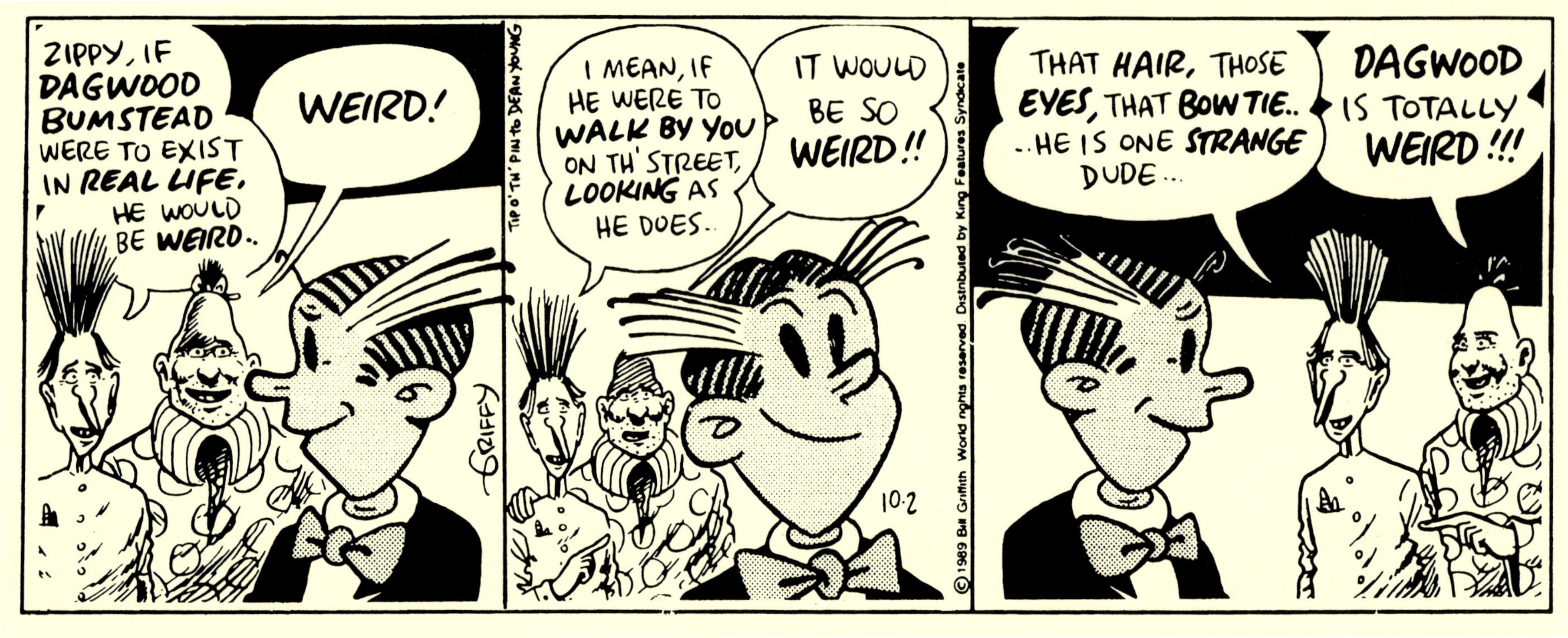
ZIPPY, IF DAGWOOD BUMSTEAD WERE TO EXIST IN REAL LIFE, HE WOULD BE WEIRD..
WEIRD!
GRIFFY
TIP O' TH' PIN to DEAN YOUNG
I MEAN, IF HE WERE TO WALK BY YOU ON TH' STREET, LOOKING AS HE DOES..
IT WOULD BE SO WEIRD!!
10·2
© 1989 Bill Griffith World rights reserved. Distributed by King Features Syndicate
THAT HAIR, THOSE EYES, THAT BOW TIE.. ..HE IS ONE STRANGE DUDE...
DAGWOOD IS TOTALLY WEIRD!!!

Bill Griffith *Zippy*
2 October 1989.
Reprinted by special permission of King Features Syndicate.

commentary on its own meaning, as when a character notes its "obscure references, elliptical sense of humor, existentialism, and dense, often demanding word balloons" (22 April 1991), or when Griffy describes Zippy as "a soulful, complex character with a Zen-like philosophy" (11 November 1992) and "a 'wise fool' whose seemingly bizarre pronouncements have a touching, almost mystical edge" (12 November 1992). Griffy then appropriately and succinctly describes the strip as a "somewhat surreal but perceptive view of the human condition" (14 November 1992).

The characters of *Zippy* find themselves revisiting the artist's boyhood and formative experiences, traveling back in time to the beginnings of the comic strip or some artistic movement, toying with cartoon anthropomorphism, and consorting with symbols from advertising and motion pictures as well as characters from other comic strip features, especially Nancy and Sluggo, Blondie and Dagwood, Popeye, Ziggy, Garfield, Mark Trail, Beetle Bailey, and the children from *Family Circus*. The language and visual imagery of *Zippy* are laced with metaphors drawn from and references to the entire history of comic strips and popular culture in general, in a self-conscious and brilliantly envisioned parody of postmodern thought in the United States.

Another recent comic strip which makes self-referentiality a basic structural principle and source of humor is *Big Nate* by Lincoln Pierce. The central character of the feature which began in 1991 is Nate Wright, an eleven-year-old aspiring cartoonist who is remarkably self-confident that his home-drawn comic strips represent works of genius. Basically, he uses the comic strip as a means of having revenge on his tough schoolteacher Mrs. Godfrey, or ridiculing others around him. While Pierce himself uses an old fashioned big-foot style of cartooning, he allows Nate a primitive style that creates an effective counterpoint to his own. The childish exaggeration of Nate's style makes Pierce's seem almost realistic by comparison and provides a wry commentary on our tolerance for comic distortion in the funnies, particularly at a time when many popular comic features, such as *Cathy* or *Sally Forth*, have not been distinguished for their draftsmanship. In some cases, the comic content and ideas can carry the art.

Very often *Big Nate* is partially or entirely turned over to one of Nate's strips drawn on a legal pad and reproduced with the ruled lines showing. Presumably Nate has not yet learned to use the basic tools of

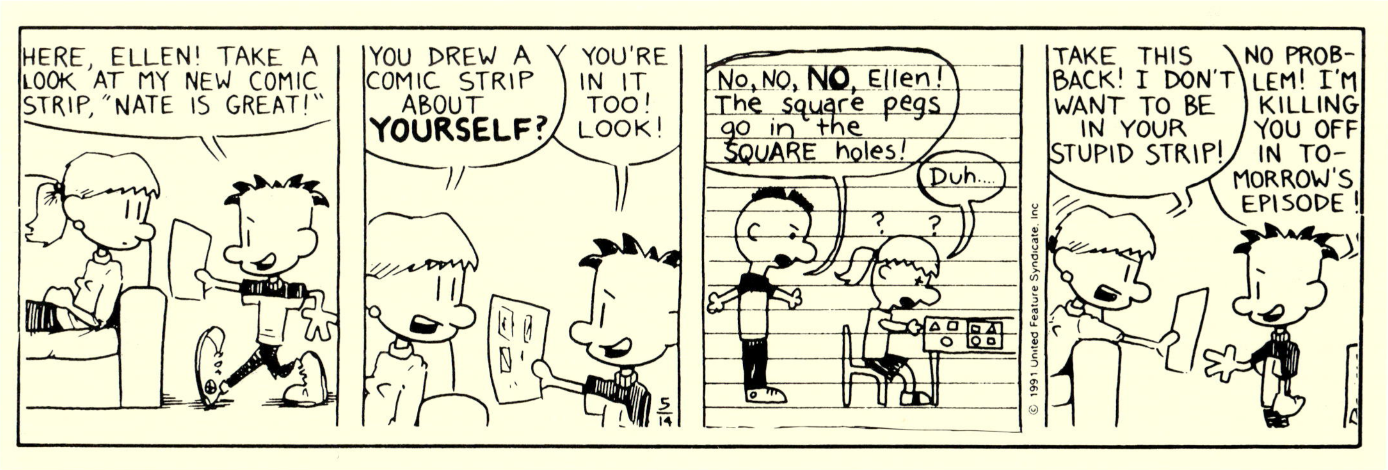
HERE, ELLEN! TAKE A LOOK AT MY NEW COMIC STRIP, "NATE IS GREAT!"
YOU DREW A COMIC STRIP ABOUT YOURSELF?
YOU'RE IN IT TOO! LOOK!
5/14
No, NO, NO, Ellen! The square pegs go in the SQUARE holes!
Duh....
© 1991 United Feature Syndicate, Inc
TAKE THIS BACK! I DON'T WANT TO BE IN YOUR STUPID STRIP!
NO PROBLEM! I'M KILLING YOU OFF IN TOMORROW'S EPISODE!

Lincoln Pierce *Big Nate*
14 May 1991.
Big Nate reprinted by permission of United Feature Syndicate, Inc.

cartooning and uses his school notebooks for doodling rather than assignments; but his mentor is, after all, Rusty Sienna, a television personality who demonstrates the art of painting unicorns on velvet during his show.

While he often features himself in his own strip, "The Adventures of Nate," in some glorious role, or his adolescent sister doing something foolish in "The Zany Escapades of Ellen," Nate has also created several continuing features, such as "Dr. Cesspool and His Faithful Nurse, Maureen Biology" and "The Adventures of Kit and Kaboodle." The first is a spoof of stories about doctors in the popular media depicting Cesspool as negligent and stupid rather than helpful and intelligent; and the second satirizes the comic book, especially Batman and Robin and similar man and boy teams inspired by their example. Thus Pierce uses one form of comic art to satirize another, an example of the kind of cross-criticism fostered by self-referentiality.

Reading *Big Nate* with appreciation and understanding requires that the reader be familiar with the entire scope of popular media. Pierce achieves two levels of humor in his feature—that of the adult world of Nate's father and teachers, and Nate's own immature humor in his crudely-drawn strips that usually feature violence and

mayhem. Both are funny for different reasons and serve to achieve Pierce's purpose: the exploration of the world of a child seeking to discover himself as his aspirations and dreams are punctured by the wisdom and experience of his elders. Somehow his ego remains intact as he makes compromises to get ahead or creatively avoid his homework. Pierce has created a delicately complex world of comic self-reflexivity. One is tempted to read a good deal of autobiography into *Big Nate* and view it as an account of the difficulties of being talented in a society that has lost touch with fantasy and imagination, not unlike *Calvin and Hobbes*.

Another character who imagines himself to be a cartoonist extraordinaire is Jason Fox in Bill Amend's family situation comedy *Fox Trot*. In a two week sequence reprinted in the anthology *Enormously Fox Trot*, Jason contributes a comic strip to the school newspaper mainly in hopes of merchandising offers rather than amusing his readers.[21] When "Squishy and Squashy, the Talking Roadkill Brothers" is rejected, he is quick to proclaim violation of his freedom of expression and identifies himself with the misunderstood avant-garde. A schoolmate muses, "I wonder if they know the lesson they are teaching," while a complacent Jason prepares to

WHAT ARE YOU DOING?
I HEARD THAT THE GUY WHO DRAWS "THE FAR SIDE" IS RETIRING AT THE END OF THE YEAR.
GARY LARSON? YEAH, I HEARD THAT TOO. SO?
WELL, I FIGURE THAT JUST BECAUSE HE'S QUITTING, IT DOESN'T MEAN THAT "THE FAR SIDE" HAS TO END. I'LL JUST TAKE IT OVER FOR HIM. I'M PUTTING TOGETHER A SAMPLE BATCH NOW.
THINK ABOUT IT! OVERNIGHT, YOUR LITTLE BROTHER COULD BECOME ONE OF THE WORLD'S MOST WIDELY READ CARTOONISTS! I'D BE FAMOUS! PEOPLE WOULD BE BEATING A PATH TO OUR DOOR!
WITH PITCHFORKS AND TORCHES, MOST LIKELY.
HEE HEE HEE– IF YOU THINK THAT ONE'S GROSS...
© 1994 B ll Amend
10-17
AMEND
Dist. by Universal Press Syndicate

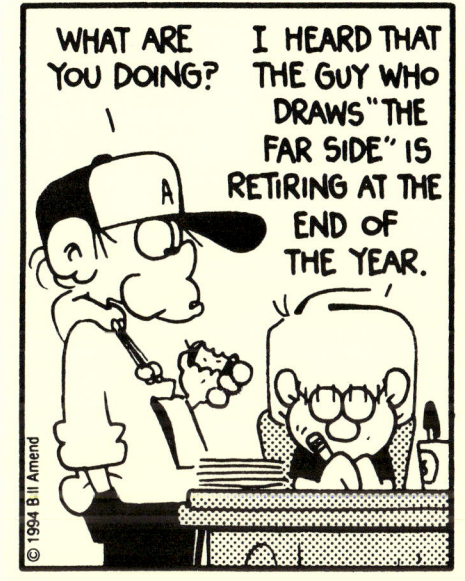

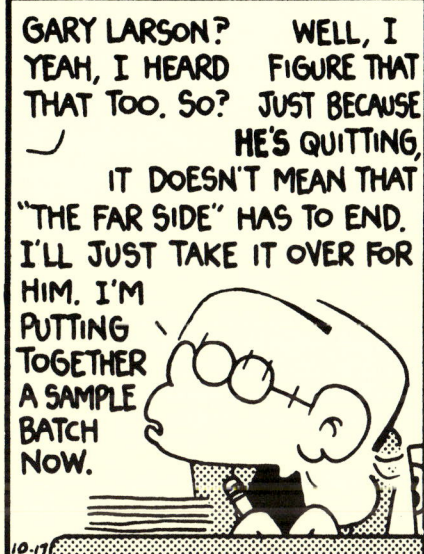

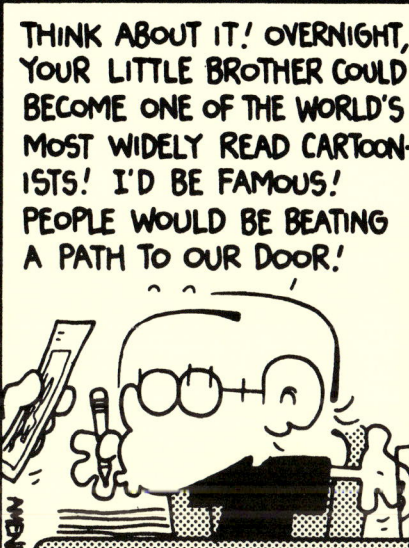

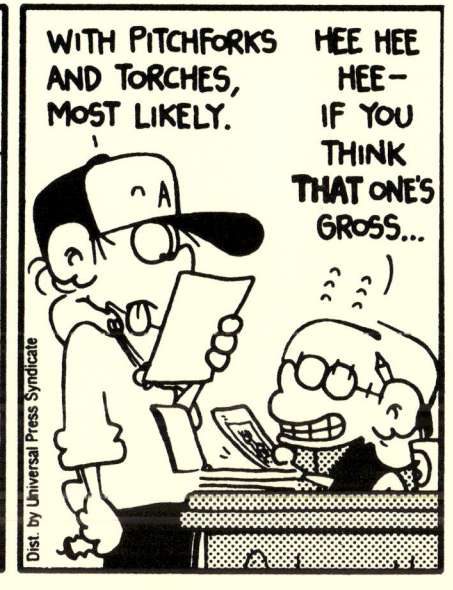

Bill Amend *FoxTrot*
17 October 1994.
Distributed by Universal Press Syndicate.

resubmit his strip, but this time with "happy jokes." So much for the artistic temperament. On another occasion, Jason spends a week producing substitute panels for *Family Circus* because he can draw "perfect circles" and Bil Keane "seems to go on vacation like a hundred times a year" leaving little Billy to fill in for his Dad.[22] When everyone finally convinces Jason that he is no Bil Keane, rather than create his own feature, he decides to "go after one of those strips where the original creator died a million years ago." Competing elements of the cartooning profession, in this case art vs. commerce and originality vs. imitation are once again subjected to satiric scrutiny through Amend's gentle wit.

Lest we conclude that metacomics are meant purely for diversion or self-indulgence, let us look at two examples of how they can be used to make serious statements about the larger scheme of things. In the 21 May 1989 Sunday *Donald Duck* page produced by a Disney studio artist, Donald and his Uncle Ludwig, the inventor, are trapped by a device which instantly moves them back in time and replays the comic strip sequence in which they appear—on into infinity, we assume. Such a strip approaches the metaphysical and suggests the mesmerizing power of the concept of infinity, where things have no conclusion and repeat themselves forever. The strip also serves as a perfect visual paradigm of the concept it expresses, a balanced four-square set of images that pull us through the never-ending sequence over and over again. Here form and content are inseparably merged.

In the 8 June 1975 Sunday page from the little-known but superb comic strip *Conchy*, Jim Childress had his character express consciousness of himself as a piece of fiction, and through commentary on the conventions of his existence, make a statement about illusion and reality. His brief disquisition merits careful consideration in its statement that the real world, like the comic strip, is but a reflection of existence and neither is more substantial nor permanent than the other. By stating the uncertainty of the meaning of life within the comics, Conchy also expresses our own insecurities about the meaning of life in our universe. As many thinkers and writers from Plato to Shakespeare have noted, life may be merely someone else's dream, perhaps a cartoonist's.

In these two instances, as Richard Alter has noted about metafiction, ". . . through a sudden glimpse of multiple possibilities of images we are brought up short and thus moved to ponder the nature of representation and the presence of the artful representer."[23] If the primary concern of metafiction is ". . . to express the novelist's vision of experience by exploring the process of its own making,"[24] then surely metacomics may share the same intention. Since self-referentiality has been central in form and function to all postmodern arts, it is not surprising that comic strips also reflect the philosophic uncertainties and self-questioning that have obsessed twentieth century culture in general. The intent of this essay has not been to say that the comics have been doing something different from what we thought, but rather more than we allowed was possible. The serious study of comics, then, may be a central element in our understanding of postmodern civilization.

HERE'S A ROUGH ONE, ZONKER! IT COMES TO US FROM J.M. OF CHEVY CHASE. "DEAR SIR: WHY DON'T YOU TURN OVER THE ILLUSTRATION TO SOMEONE WITH SOME DRAWING SKILLS?"
12-30
UNIVERSAL PRESS SYNDICATE © 1992 G.B. Trudeau
WELL, J.M., WHAT YOUR HURTFUL LETTER DOESN'T ACKNOWLEDGE IS HOW FAR THIS FEATURE HAS COME! TAKE A LOOK AT THE FIRST DAY OF SYNDICATION!
HI THERE! MY NAME'S MIKE DOONESBURY. I HAIL FROM TULSA, OKLAHOMA AND WOMEN ADORE ME! GLAD TO MEET YOU, ROOMIE!
SO YOU SEE, IT COULD BE WORSE...
I DUNNO, I SORT OF PREFER THAT PERIOD.
GB Trudeau

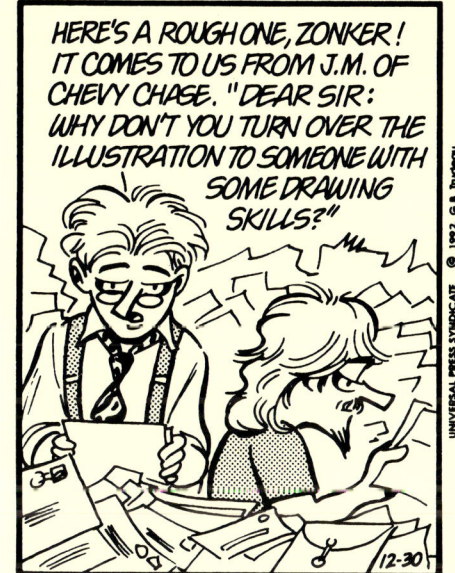

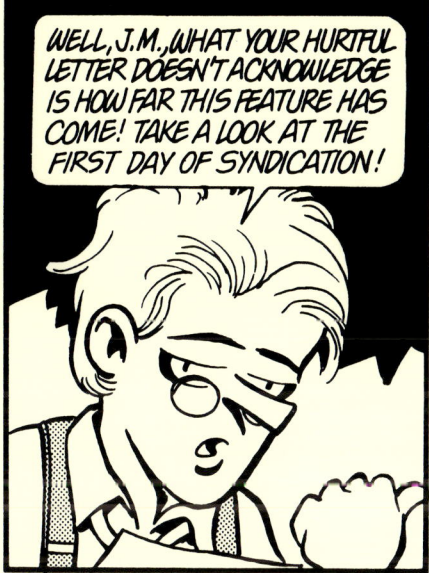

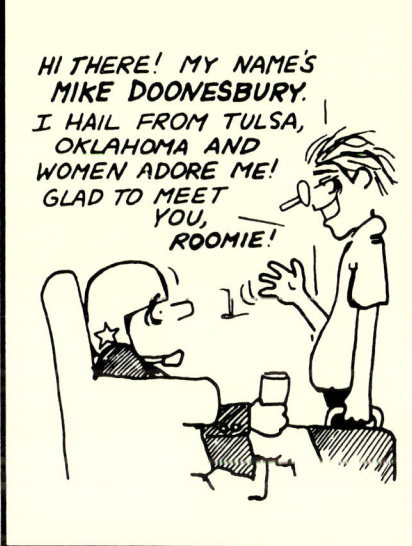

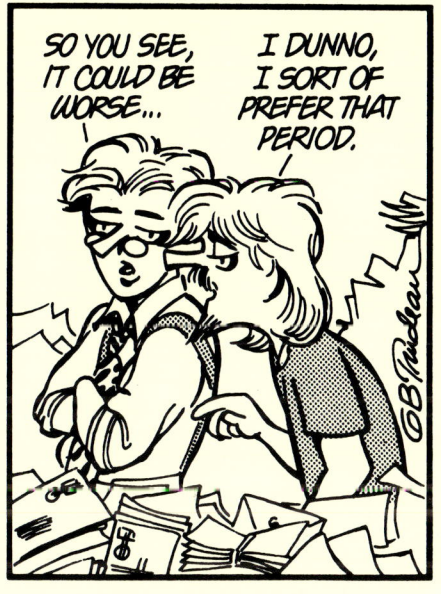

Garry Trudeau *Doonesbury*
30 December 1992.
Distributed by
Universal Press Syndicate.

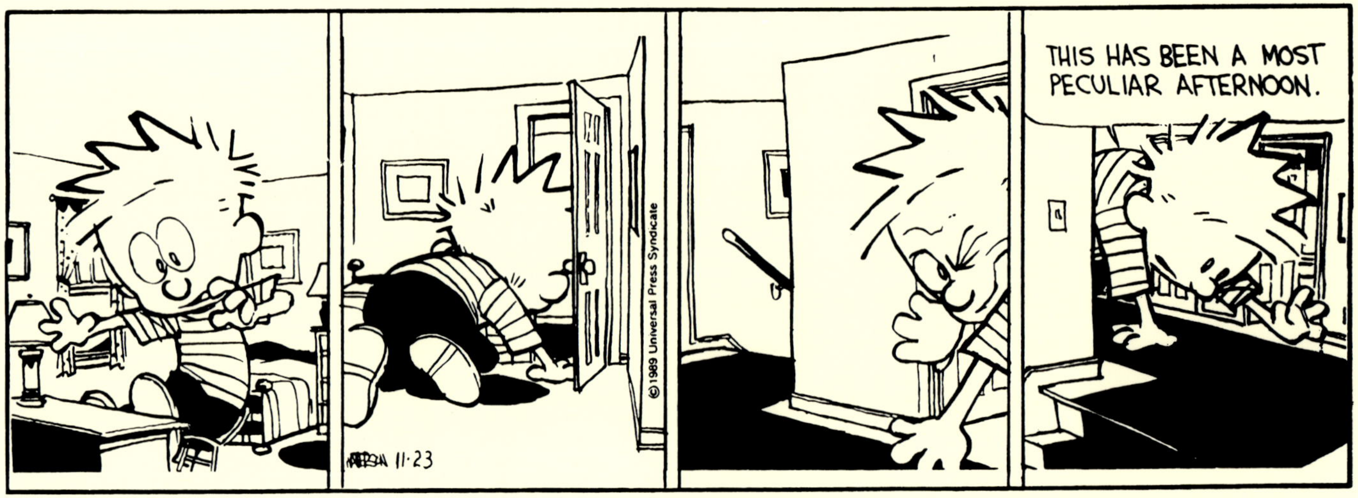
©1989 Universal Press Syndicate
THIS HAS BEEN A MOST PECULIAR AFTERNOON.

Bill Watterson *Calvin and Hobbes*
23 November 1989.
Distributed by Universal Press Syndicate.

NOTES

1. Some of the material in this essay appeared in a different form in "Form and Function in Metacomics: Self-Reflexivity in the Comic Strips," *Studies in Popular Culture* 13:2 (1991), 1-10.
2. Reprinted in Richard F. Outcault, *Buster Brown: Early Strips in Full Color* (New York: Dover, 1987), 29-30.
3. Reprinted in Maurice Horn, *75 Years of the Comics* (Boston: Boston Book & Art, 1971), 30.
4. Reprinted in *Winsor McCay's Dream Days*. ed. Bill Blackbeard (Westport, CT: Hyperion, 1977), 111.
5. Interview with the author, 21 January 1994, Santa Rosa, CA.
6. Charles Perrault, *Perrault's Fairy Tales* (New York: Dover, 1969), 113 and 117.
7. *The Annotated Alice*, Martin Gardiner, ed. (New York: Clarkson N. Potter, 1960), 186.
8. *More Annotated Alice*, Martin Gardiner, ed. (New York: Random House, 1990), 170.
9. Reprinted in *Screw Ball Comics/Nemo Annual No. 1*, ed. Richard Marshall (Thousand Oaks, CA: Fantagraphics Books, 1985), 16.
10. Quoted in Ron Goulart, *Encyclopedia of American Comics* (New York: Facts on File, 1990), 340.
11. Reprinted in Al Capp, *Li'l Abner: Dailies*, vol. 10 (Princeton, WI: Kitchen Sink Press, 1990), 8.
12. E.J. Kahn, Jr. "Oof!! (Sob!) Eep!! (Gulp!) Zowie!!!" *The New Yorker*, 29 November 1947, 45.
13. Max Allan Collins, "The Strip Within a Strip," in Al Capp, *Li'l Abner: Dailies*, vol. 10, 11.
14. Described in "Li'l Abner's Mad Capp, " *Newsweek*, 24 November 1947, 63.
15. "Writ by Hand," *Newsweek*, 3 June 1946. 58.
16. Both Steinbeck's and Chaplin's appreciations are reprinted as prefaces to Al Capp, *The World of Li'l Abner* (New York: Ballantine Books, 1952). Steinbeck called Capp "the best writer in America."
17. Quoted in David Schreiner, "The Beginnings of a Roll . . .," *The Spirit*, June 1986, inside front cover.
18. Brian Walker, *The Best of Ernie Bushmiller's Nancy* (New York: Comicana Books/Henry Holt, 1988), 91.
19. Walker, *The Best of Ernie Bushmiller's Nancy*, 91.
20. Walker, *The Best of Ernie Bushmiller's Nancy*, 98.
21. Bill Amend, *Enormously FoxTrot: A FoxTrot Treasury* (Kansas City, MO: Andrews and McMeel, 1994), 98, 218-222.
22. Amend, *Enormously FoxTrot: A FoxTrot Treasury*, 125-126.
23. Richard Alter, *Partial Magic: The Novel as a Self-Conscious Genre* (Berkeley: University of California Press, 1975), 8.
24. Inger Christensen, *The Meaning of Metafiction* (Bergen and Oslo: Universitetsforlager, 1981), 11.

SELECTED BIBLIOGRAPHY

Alter, Richard. *Partial Magic: The Novel as a Self-Conscious Genre*. Berkeley: University of California Press, 1975.

Amend, Bill. *Enormously FoxTrot: A FoxTrot Treasury*. Kansas City, MO: Andrews and McMeel, 1994.

Capp, Al. *Li'l Abner*. 20 vols. Northampton, MA: Kitchen Sink Press, 1988- (Complete reprinting in forty-three volumes in progress.)

____. *Fearless Fosdick*. Princeton, WI: Kitchen Sink Press, 1990.

____. *Fearless Fosdick*: The Hole Story. Princeton, WI: Kitchen Sink Press, 1992.

Chambers, Ross. *Story and Situation: Narrative Seduction and the Power of Fiction*. Minneapolis: University of Minnesota Press, 1984.

Christensen, Inger. *The Meaning of Metafiction*. Bergen and Oslo: Universitetsforlaget, 1981.

Dunne, Michael. *Metapop: Self-Referentiality in Contemporary American Popular Culture*. Jackson: University Press of Mississippi, 1992.

Eisner, Will. "Li'l Adam the Stupid Mountain Boy." *The Spirit*, issue 20 (June 1986), 9-15. [Reprint of 20 July 1947 episode of *The Spirit*.]

Federman, Raymond, ed. *Surfiction: Fiction Now . . . and Tomorrow*. Chicago: Swallow Press, 1975.

Fisher, Bud. *A. Mutt*. Westport, CT: Hyperion Press, 1977.

Gaggi, Silvio. *Modern/Postmodern: A Study in Twentieth-Century Arts and Ideas*. Philadelphia: University of Pennsylvania Press, 1989.

Galewitz, Herb, ed. *Bringing Up Father by Geo. McManus*. New York: Scribner's, 1973.

Gardner, Martin, ed. *The Annotated Alice*. New York: Clarkson N. Potter, 1960.

____. *More Annotated Alice*. New York: Random House, 1990.

Goulart, Ron, ed. *The Encyclopedia of American Comics*. New York: Facts on File, 1990.

Hutcheon, Linda. *A Poetics of Postmodernism: History, Theory, Fiction*. New York: Routledge, 1988.

____. *Narcissistic Narrative: The Metafictional Paradox*. New York: Methuen, 1980.

Inge, M. Thomas. "'Metacomics' That Self-Consciously Joke about the Limits of the Art Form." *Chronicle of Higher Education*, 16 May 1990, B56.

____. *Great American Comics: 100 Years of Cartoon Art*. Washington, DC: Smithsonian Institution Traveling Exhibition Service, 1990.

Kahn, E. J., Jr. "Ooff!! (Sob!) Eep!! (Gulp!) Zowie!!!" *The New Yorker*, 29 November 1947, 45-55; and 6 December 1947, 46-59. [Profile of Al Capp]

Kurtzman, Harvey. *Hey Look.* Princeton, WI: Kitchen Sink Press, 1992.

"Li'l Abner's Mad Capp." *Newsweek*, 24 November 1947, 60-63.

McCay, Winsor. *Winsor McCay's Dream Days.* Westport, CT: Hyperion Press, 1977.

Outcault, Richard F. *Buster Brown.* New York: Dover, 1974.

Overstreet, Robert M. *The Overstreet Comic Book Price Guide.* 25th ed. New York: Avon Books, 1995.

Perrault, Charles. *Perrault's Fairy Tales.* New York: Dover, 1969.

Pierce, Lincoln. *Awesome Big Nate Comics.* New York: Avon Books, 1993.

Schreiner, Dave. "The Beginnings of a Roll . . . " *The Spirit*, issue 20 (June 1986), inside front cover, 32, inside back cover.

Screw Ball Comics/Nemo Annual 1. Richard Marschall, ed. Thousand Oaks, CA: Fantagraphics Books, 1985.

Walker, Brian. *The Best of Ernie Bushmiller's Nancy.* New York: Comicana Books/Henry Holt, 1988.

Walker, Mort. *The Lexicon of Comicana.* Port Chester, NY: Museum of Cartoon Art, 1980.

____ and Jerry Dumas. *Sam's Strip Lives.* Greenwich, CT: Carriage House, 1963.

"Writ by Hand." *Newsweek*, 3 June 1946, 58. [Al Capp]

"Yokum Gold." *Newsweek*, 21 July 1947, 54. [Al Capp and Will Eisner]

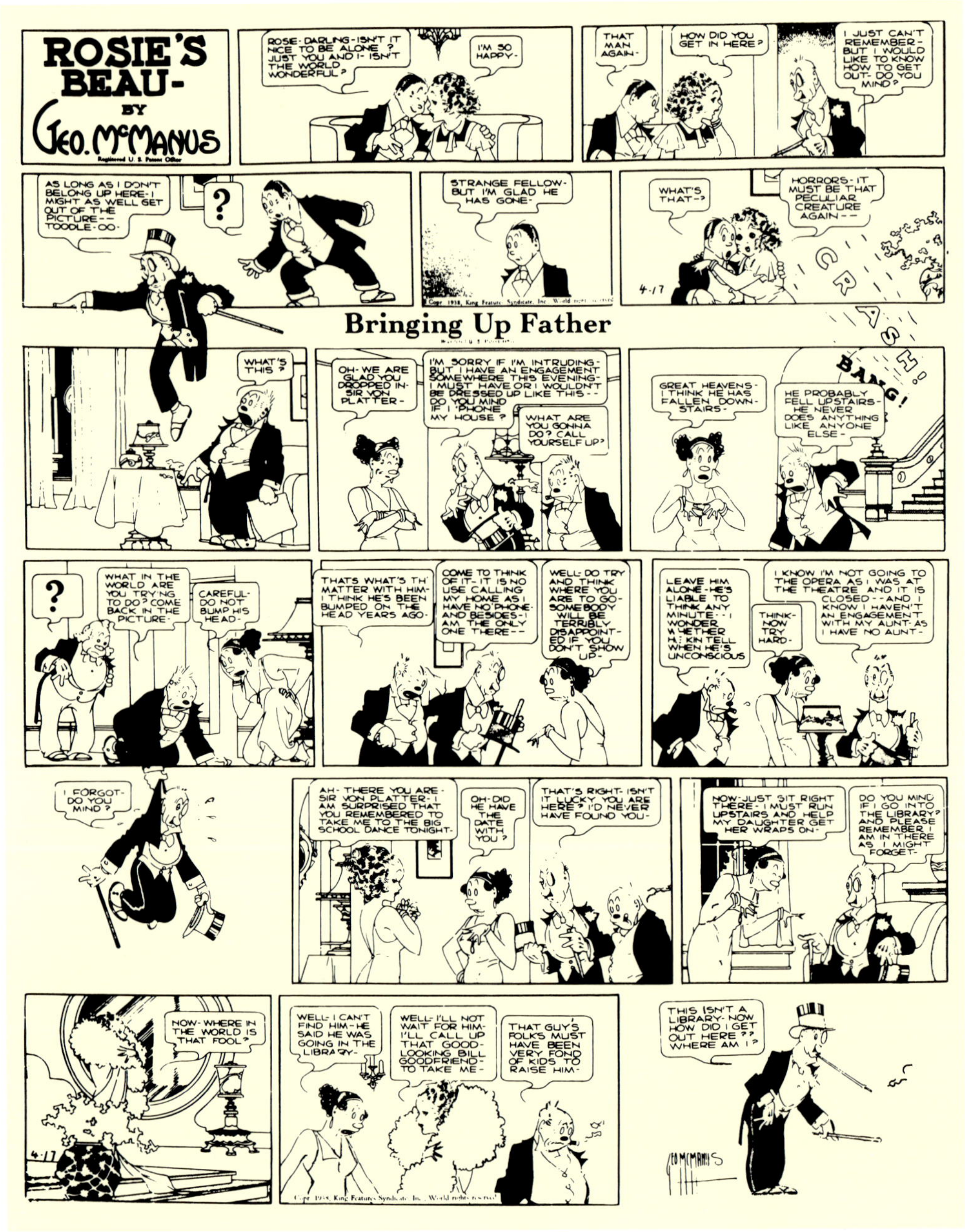

ROSIE'S BEAU- BY GEO. McMANUS
Registered U. S. Patent Office
ROSE- DARLING- ISN'T IT NICE TO BE ALONE ? JUST YOU AND I- ISN'T THE WORLD WONDERFUL ?
I'M SO HAPPY-
THAT MAN AGAIN-
HOW DID YOU GET IN HERE ?
I JUST CAN'T REMEMBER- BUT I WOULD LIKE TO KNOW HOW TO GET OUT- DO YOU MIND ?
AS LONG AS I DON'T BELONG UP HERE- I MIGHT AS WELL GET OUT OF THE PICTURE-- TOODLE-OO-
?
STRANGE FELLOW- BUT I'M GLAD HE HAS GONE-
WHAT'S THAT-?
HORRORS- IT MUST BE THAT PECULIAR CREATURE AGAIN--
CRASH!
4-17
Bringing Up Father
WHAT'S THIS ?
OH- WE ARE GLAD YOU DROPPED IN- SIR VON PLATTER-
I'M SORRY IF I'M INTRUDING- BUT I HAVE AN ENGAGEMENT SOMEWHERE THIS EVENING- I MUST HAVE OR I WOULDN'T BE DRESSED UP LIKE THIS-- DO YOU MIND IF I 'PHONE MY HOUSE ?
WHAT ARE YOU GONNA DO ? CALL YOURSELF UP ?
BANG!
GREAT HEAVENS- I THINK HE HAS FALLEN DOWN-STAIRS-
HE PROBABLY FELL UPSTAIRS- HE NEVER DOES ANYTHING LIKE ANYONE ELSE-
?
WHAT IN THE WORLD ARE YOU TRY'NG TO DO ? COME BACK IN THE PICTURE-
CAREFUL- DO NOT BUMP HIS HEAD-
THATS WHAT'S TH' MATTER WITH HIM- I THINK HE'S BEEN BUMPED ON THE HEAD YEARS AGO-
COME TO THINK OF IT- IT IS NO USE CALLING MY HOME AS I HAVE NO 'PHONE- AND BESIDES- I AM THE ONLY ONE THERE--
WELL- DO TRY AND THINK WHERE YOU ARE TO GO- SOMEBODY WILL BE TERRIBLY DISAPPOINTED IF YOU DON'T SHOW UP-
LEAVE HIM ALONE- HE'S LIABLE TO THINK ANY MINUTE-- I WONDER WHETHER H: KIN TELL WHEN HE'S UNCONSCIOUS
THINK- NOW TRY HARD-
I KNOW I'M NOT GOING TO THE OPERA AS I WAS AT THE THEATRE AND IT IS CLOSED-- AND I KNOW I HAVEN'T AN ENGAGEMENT WITH MY AUNT- AS I HAVE NO AUNT-
I FORGOT- DO YOU MIND ?
AH- THERE YOU ARE- SIR VON PLATTER- I AM SURPRISED THAT YOU REMEMBERED TO TAKE ME TO THE BIG SCHOOL DANCE TONIGHT-
OH- DID HE HAVE THE DATE WITH YOU ?
THAT'S RIGHT- ISN'T IT LUCKY YOU ARE HERE ? I'D NEVER HAVE FOUND YOU-
NOW- JUST SIT RIGHT THERE- I MUST RUN UPSTAIRS AND HELP MY DAUGHTER GET HER WRAPS ON-
DO YOU MIND IF I GO INTO THE LIBRARY ? AND PLEASE REMEMBER I AM IN THERE AS I MIGHT FORGET-
NOW- WHERE IN THE WORLD IS THAT FOOL ?
4-17
WELL- I CAN'T FIND HIM- HE SAID HE WAS GOING IN THE LIBRARY-
WELL- I'LL NOT WAIT FOR HIM- I'LL CALL UP THAT GOOD-LOOKING BILL GOODFRIEND- TO TAKE ME-
THAT GUY'S FOLKS MUST HAVE BEEN VERY FOND OF KIDS TO RAISE HIM-
THIS ISN'T A LIBRARY- NOW HOW DID I GET OUT HERE ?? WHERE AM I ?
GEO McMANUS

George McManus *Rosie's Beau* and *Bringing Up Father*
17 April 1938.
Reprinted by special permission of King Features Syndicate.

APPENDIX

Will Eisner   "Li'l Adam, the Stupid Mountain Boy,"
The Spirit, 20 July 1947.
©1974 Will Eisner.
Reprinted by permission.

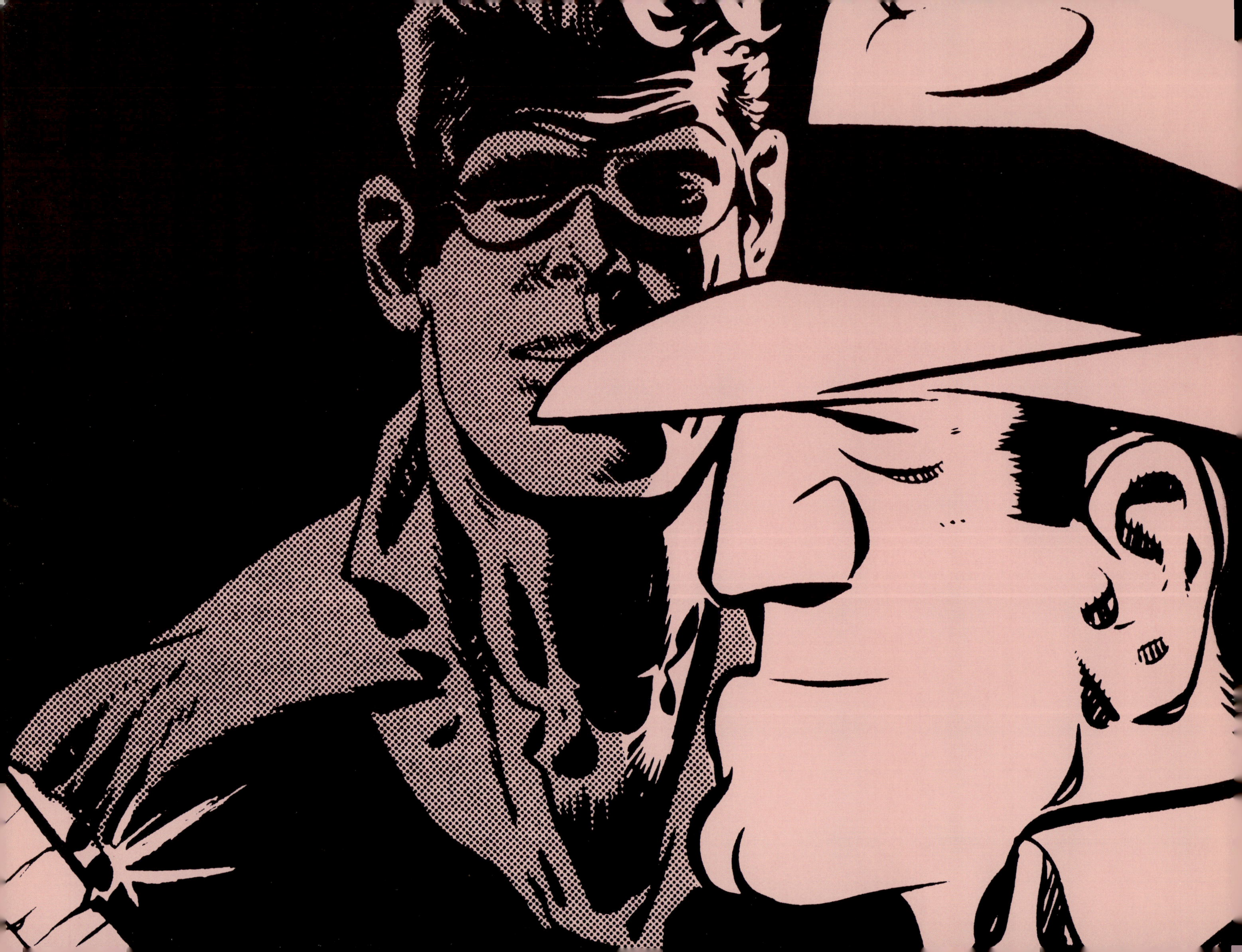

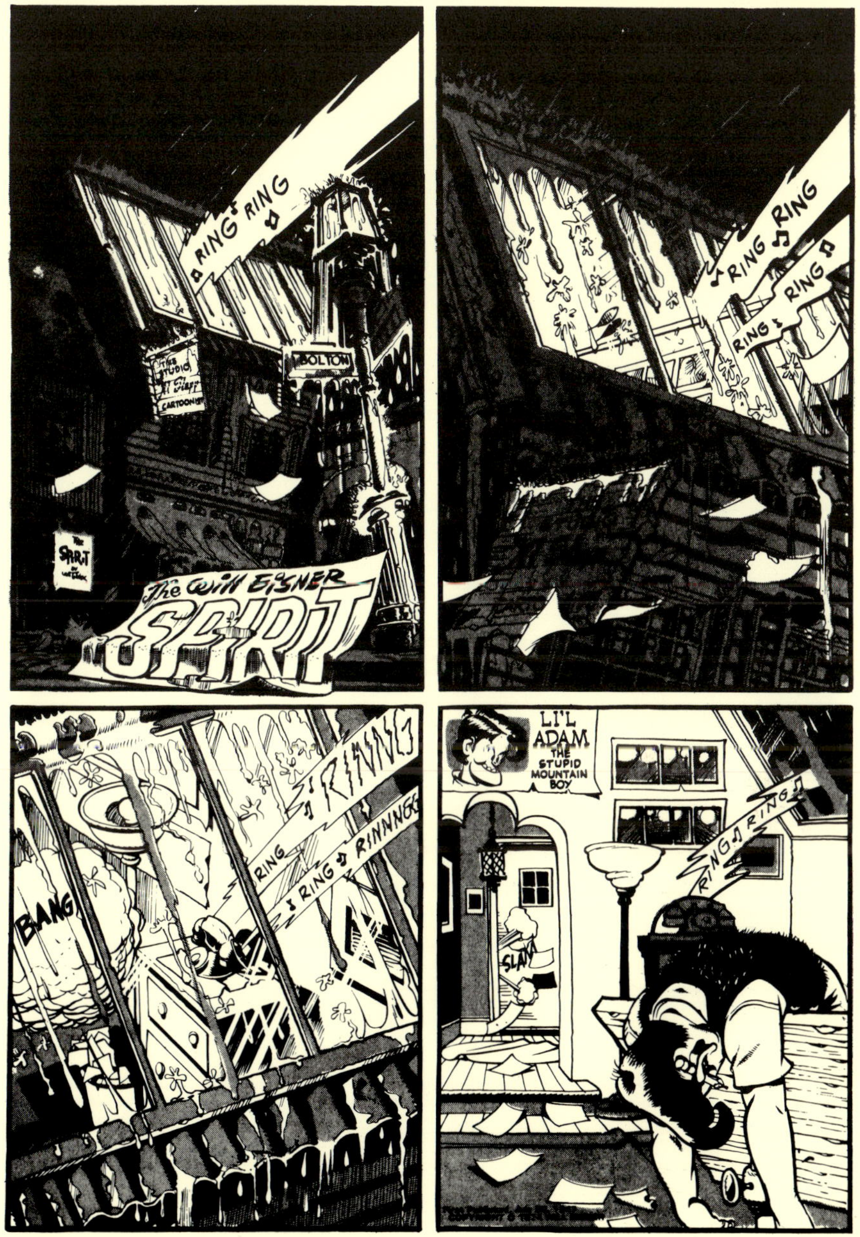
RING RING
BOLTON
CARTOONIST
The SPIRIT
The Will Eisner
SPIRIT
RING RING
RING RING
RING RING
RINNNG
RING RINNNGG
BANG
LI'L ADAM THE STUPID MOUNTAIN BOY
RING RING
SLAM

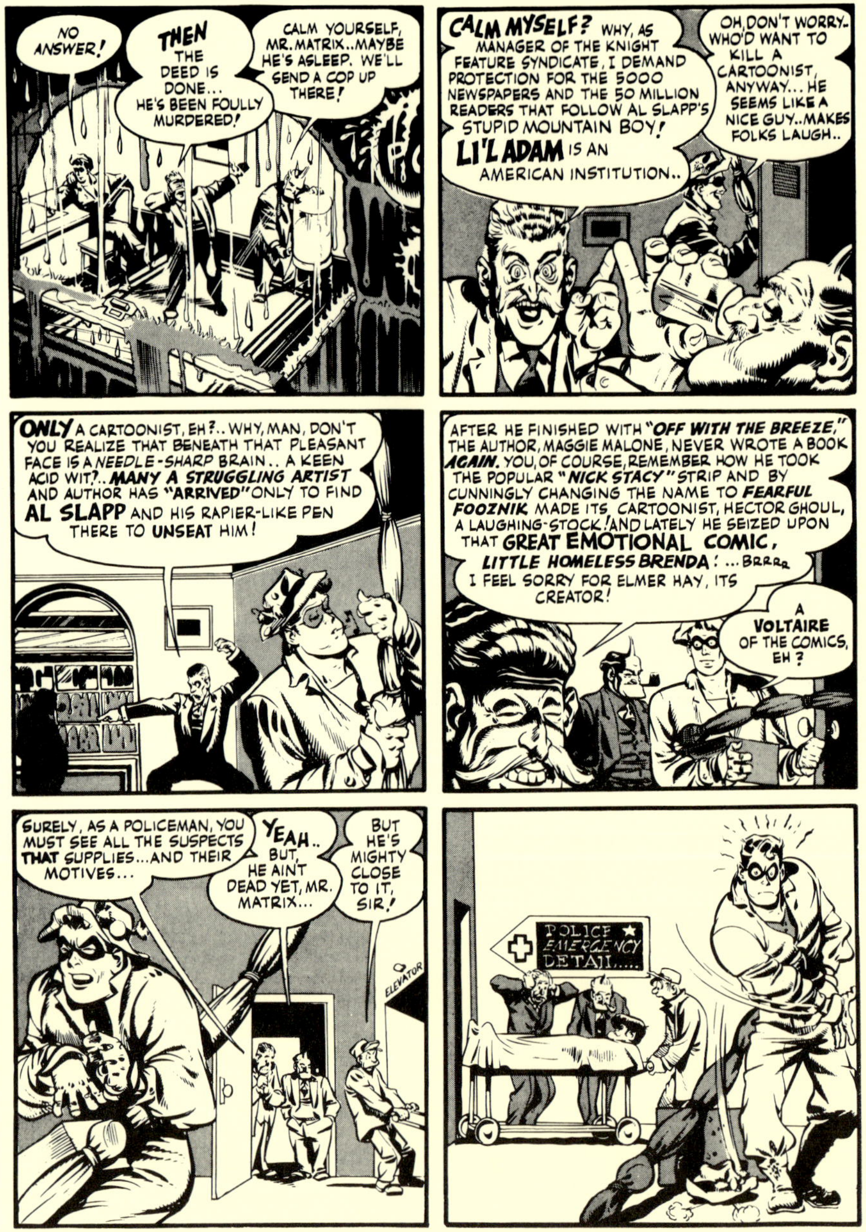
NO ANSWER!
THEN THE DEED IS DONE... HE'S BEEN FOULLY MURDERED!
CALM YOURSELF, MR. MATRIX.. MAYBE HE'S ASLEEP. WE'LL SEND A COP UP THERE!
CALM MYSELF? WHY, AS MANAGER OF THE KNIGHT FEATURE SYNDICATE, I DEMAND PROTECTION FOR THE 5000 NEWSPAPERS AND THE 50 MILLION READERS THAT FOLLOW AL SLAPP'S STUPID MOUNTAIN BOY! LI'L ADAM IS AN AMERICAN INSTITUTION..
OH, DON'T WORRY-- WHO'D WANT TO KILL A CARTOONIST, ANYWAY... HE SEEMS LIKE A NICE GUY.. MAKES FOLKS LAUGH..
ONLY A CARTOONIST, EH?.. WHY, MAN, DON'T YOU REALIZE THAT BENEATH THAT PLEASANT FACE IS A NEEDLE-SHARP BRAIN.. A KEEN ACID WIT?.. MANY A STRUGGLING ARTIST AND AUTHOR HAS "ARRIVED" ONLY TO FIND AL SLAPP AND HIS RAPIER-LIKE PEN THERE TO UNSEAT HIM!
AFTER HE FINISHED WITH "OFF WITH THE BREEZE," THE AUTHOR, MAGGIE MALONE, NEVER WROTE A BOOK AGAIN. YOU, OF COURSE, REMEMBER HOW HE TOOK THE POPULAR "NICK STACY" STRIP AND BY CUNNINGLY CHANGING THE NAME TO FEARFUL FOOZNIK MADE ITS CARTOONIST, HECTOR GHOUL, A LAUGHING-STOCK! AND LATELY HE SEIZED UPON THAT GREAT EMOTIONAL COMIC, LITTLE HOMELESS BRENDA! ... BRRRR I FEEL SORRY FOR ELMER HAY, ITS CREATOR!
A VOLTAIRE OF THE COMICS, EH?
SURELY, AS A POLICEMAN, YOU MUST SEE ALL THE SUSPECTS THAT SUPPLIES... AND THEIR MOTIVES...
YEAH.. BUT, HE AINT DEAD YET, MR. MATRIX...
BUT HE'S MIGHTY CLOSE TO IT, SIR!
ELEVATOR
POLICE EMERGENCY DETAIL....

NOW, MR. MATRIX, WHILE THE SPIRIT CHECKS FOR CLUES... GIVE ME THE ADDRESSES OF ELMER HAY AND HECTOR GHOUL.
IT'S A BAD WOUND, MR. SPIRIT, BUT HE'LL LIVE... NO SIGNS OF A STRUGGLE.. HE GOT IT FROM BEHIND..
HMM.. DON'T LET ANY NEWS LEAK OUT UNTIL I GET BACK HERE.
LATER
FIND A CLUE YET, MR. SPIRIT?
ER..NO..JUST KEEP EVERYONE OUT UNTIL YOU HEAR FROM DOLAN.
LITTLE HOMELESS BRENDA
A FEW MINUTES LATER...
ELMER HAY
YES..?
WELL! MUDDY OVERSHOES.. A WET UMBRELLA.. BEEN OUT IN THE RAIN TONIGHT, EH, MR. HAY?
URF!
LOOK HERE.. IF YOU'RE GOING TO TRY TO PIN A MURDER RAP ON ME..
MURDER?
HOW DID YOU KNOW SLAPP WAS MURDERED?
I.. THAT IS I..
A .38 PISTOL... THIS SLUG I FOUND IN SLAPP'S DRAWING BOARD WAS FROM A .38... HMMMM..
LEAPING SNAILS THIS IS A FRAME UP!
YES, MAJOR ..ANOTHER REVOLUTIONARY.. OH NO, MAJOR, I'M TAKING CARE OF HIM.. THE FOOL DOESN'T EVEN KNOW I USE GOLDEN BULLETS.. LEAD BULLETS, INDEED!

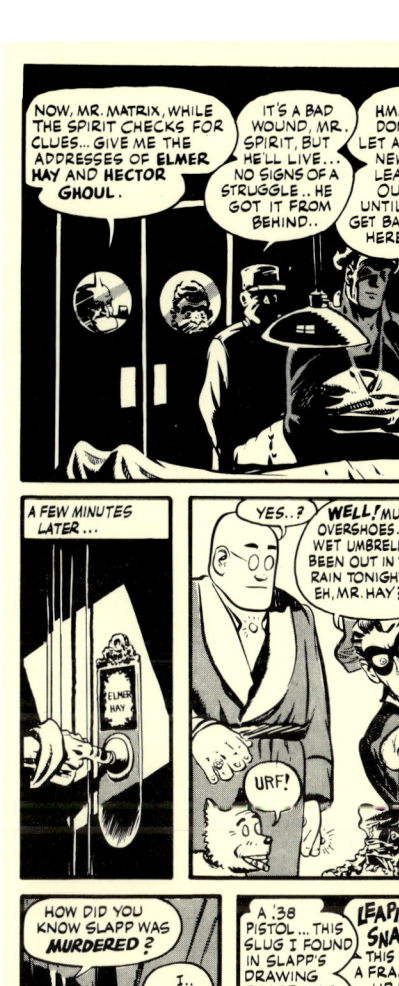

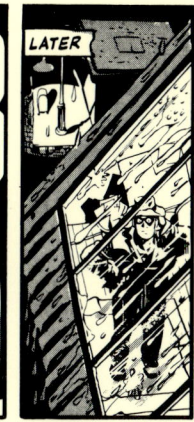

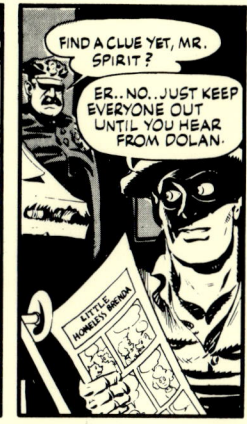

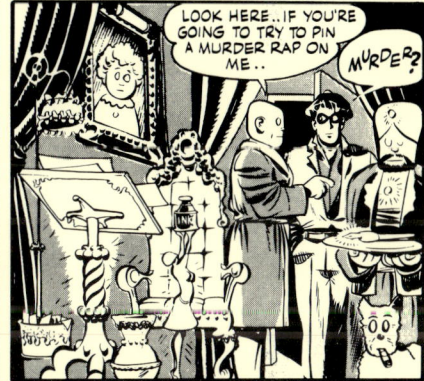

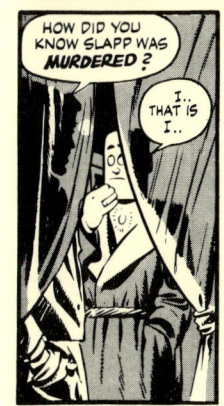

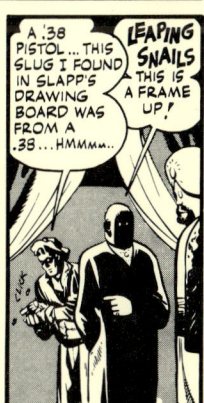

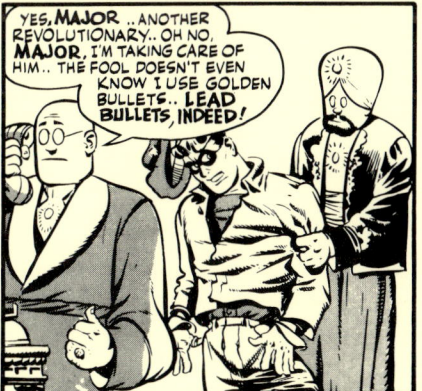

GET OUT, YOU FOREIGNER!
IN A MOMENT, BUSTER.. NOW STOP ANNOYING ME..
EEOW! I'M GOING BLIND!
..BUT MAJOR McDORNICK, I CAN'T HAVE A LOVABLE LITTLE TYKE LIKE HOMELESS BRENDA DISCUSS THE POLITICAL SITUATION.. HEY
FAR AWAY...
HAY... HELLO, HAY! CONFOUND IT! THE MAN HUNG UP ON ME!..HE ACTUALLY HUNG UP ON HOBART D. McDORNICK, THE GREAT JOURNALISTIC TYCOON!
MAYBE HE'S GOT A BETTER OFFER FROM YOUR RIVAL, RICHARD HEADLINE SMIRCH..ER, HE'S BEEN KNOWN TO STEAL A CARTOONIST NOW AND THEN!..
BACK AT ELMER HAY'S STUDIO..
NO..NO...DON'T CALL THE COPS... I DIDN'T KILL SLAPP.. WHY, THE ONLY TIME PEOPLE READ HOMELESS BRENDA IS WHEN HE DEIGNS TO MENTION HER IN HIS STRIP!
THEN WHAT WERE YOU DOING OUT IN THE RAIN TONIGHT?
HELLO... THIS IS POLICE HEADQUARTERS
...I WAS OUT DELIVERING FREE COPIES TO THE OLD LADIES' HOME! I'VE BEEN FOOLING THE MAJOR ALL THESE YEARS...Y'SEE, THEY'RE THE ONLY ONES WHO WRITE ME FAN MAIL!
DOLAN... HAS SLAPP REVIVED YET? HAY IS CLEAR, BUT I'VE GOT A NEW ANGLE ON THIS CASE!
NO! SLAPP IS STILL OUT..I'M HOLDING MATRIX UNTIL YOU GET HERE!

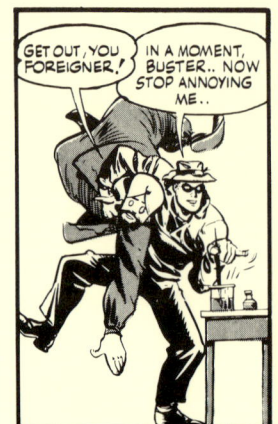

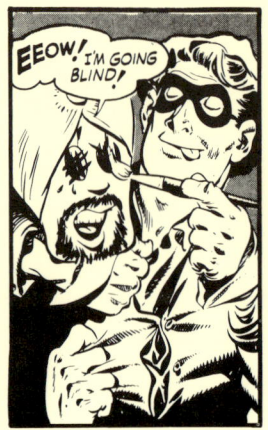

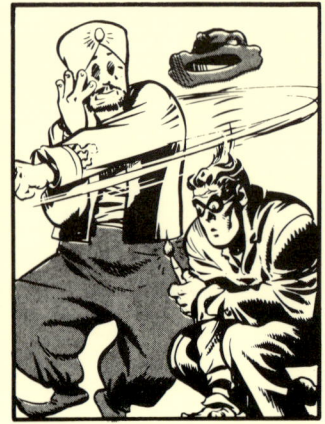

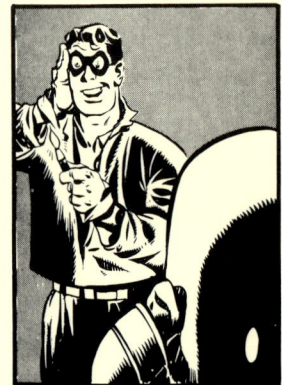

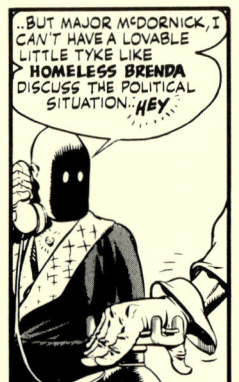

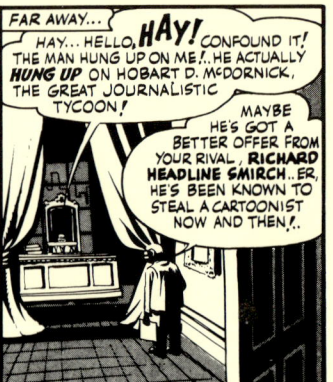

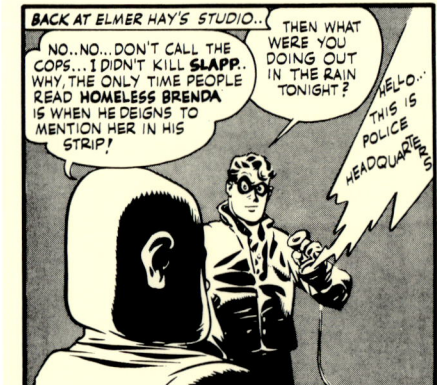

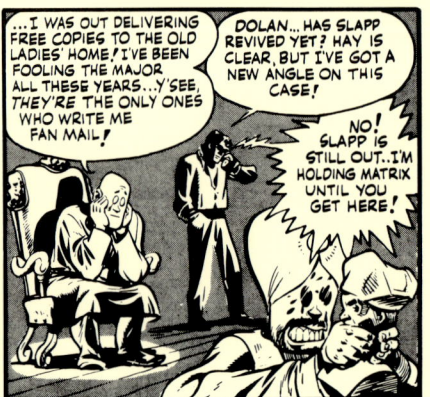

LATER..POLICE HEADQUARTERS—
HOW'D YOU MAKE SURE ELMER HAY WAS INNOCENT?
HAY USES GOLDEN BULLETS.. HE HAD NO MOTIVE..AND BESIDES HE DRAWS CHIEFLY WITH A PEN AND BLUNT BRUSHES..
WHAT'S THAT GOT TO DO WITH IT?
SLAPP WAS STABBED IN THE NECK WITH A POINTED BRUSH DIPPED IN BLACK ASPHALTUM!
...WHY, THAT STUFF IS USED IN ENGRAVING...
EGG-ZACKLY! AFTER THE DEED WAS DONE, IT WAS WASHED IN BLACK TURPENTINE AND BECAME A NORMAL BRUSH AGAIN!
CLEVER! THE MURDER INSTRUMENT DISAPPEARS... POOF
THAT SHOULD PROVE IT WAS HECTOR GHOUL!
I'LL CHECK ON THAT RIGHT NOW!
LATER..
HMM.. A POORER NEIGHBORHOOD..
GHOUL DOESN'T LIVE HERE ANY MORE.. TRY THIS ADDRESS...
NAH! GHOUL WAS KICKED OUTTA HERE..HE COULDN'T PAY THE RENT.. TRY THIS ADDRESS...
HMM.. IN THE SLUMS!
UGH! WHAT A POVERTY-STRICKEN DIVE!
COME IN...
OOOWW

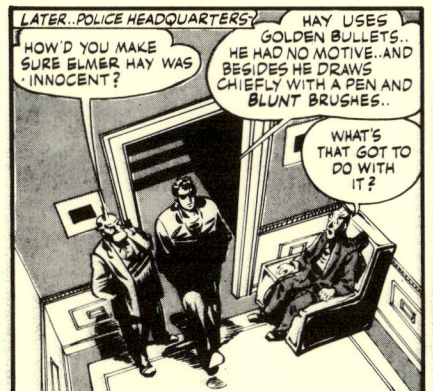

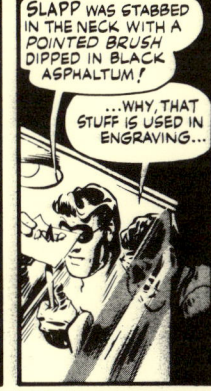

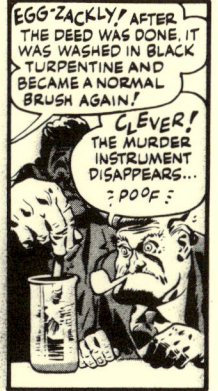

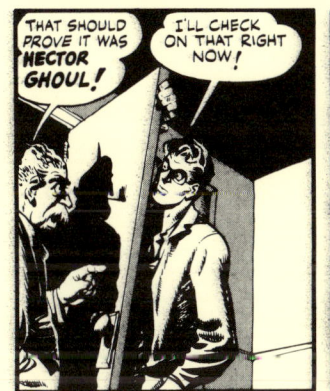

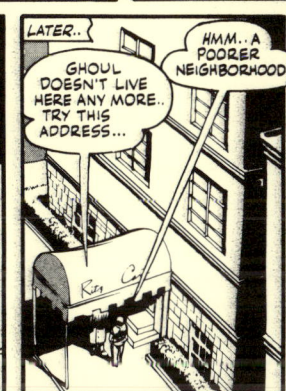

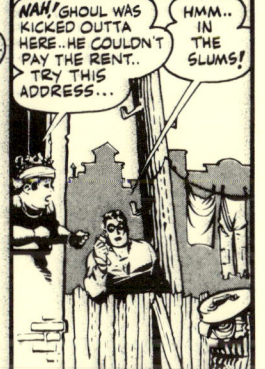

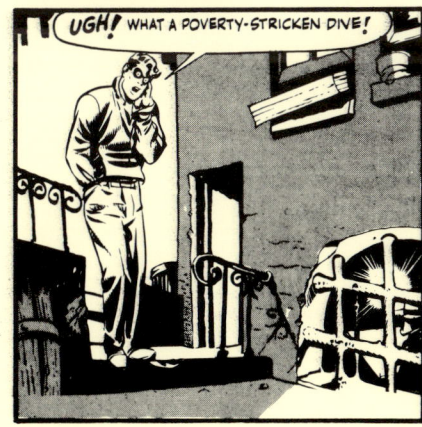

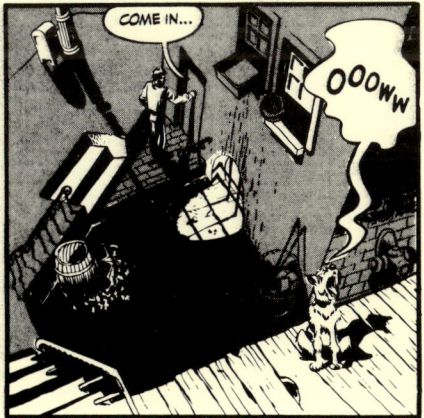

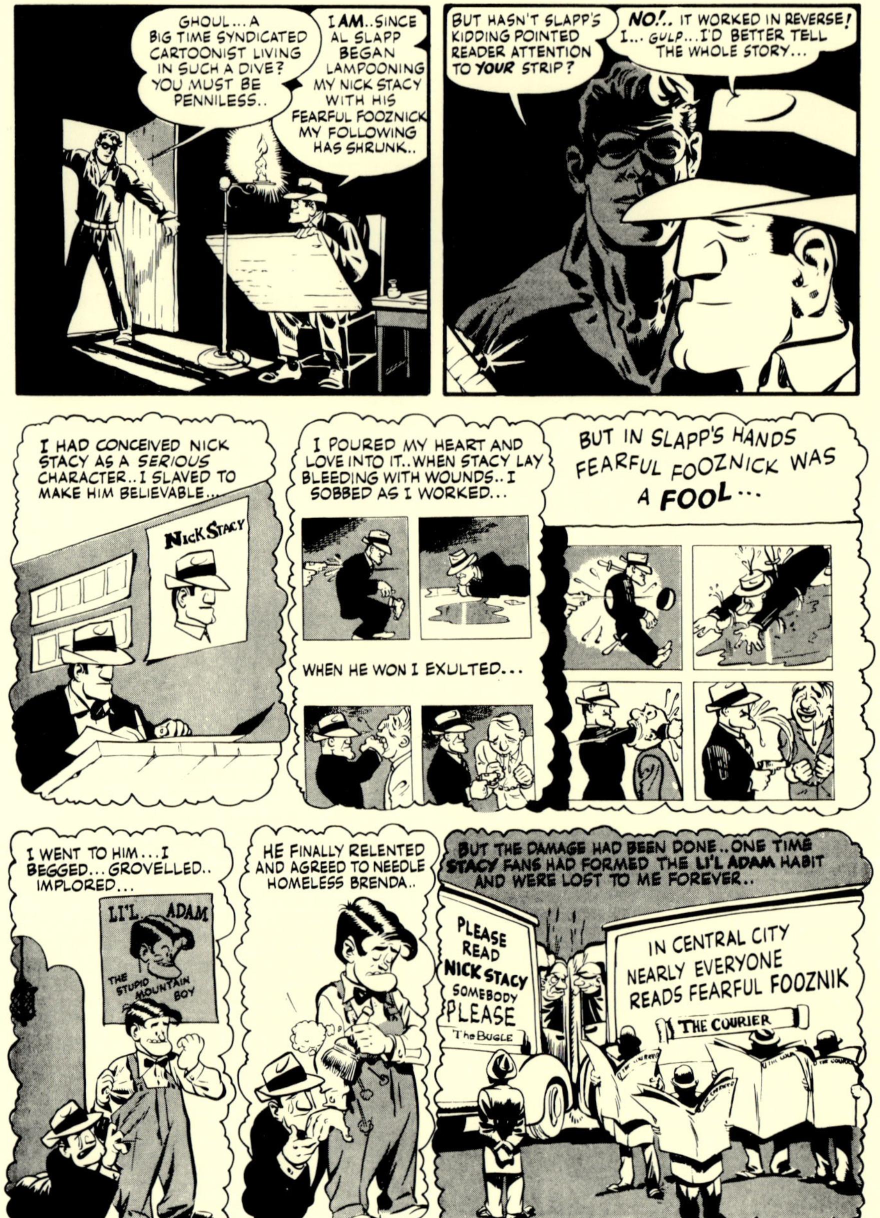
GHOUL... A BIG TIME SYNDICATED CARTOONIST LIVING IN SUCH A DIVE? YOU MUST BE PENNILESS..
I AM..SINCE AL SLAPP BEGAN LAMPOONING MY NICK STACY WITH HIS FEARFUL FOOZNICK MY FOLLOWING HAS SHRUNK..
BUT HASN'T SLAPP'S KIDDING POINTED READER ATTENTION TO YOUR STRIP?
NO!.. IT WORKED IN REVERSE! I... GULP...I'D BETTER TELL THE WHOLE STORY...
I HAD CONCEIVED NICK STACY AS A SERIOUS CHARACTER..I SLAVED TO MAKE HIM BELIEVABLE...
NICK STACY
I POURED MY HEART AND LOVE INTO IT..WHEN STACY LAY BLEEDING WITH WOUNDS..I SOBBED AS I WORKED...
WHEN HE WON I EXULTED...
BUT IN SLAPP'S HANDS FEARFUL FOOZNICK WAS A FOOL...
I WENT TO HIM...I BEGGED... GROVELLED.. IMPLORED...
LI'L ADAM
THE STUDIO MOUNTAIN BOY
HE FINALLY RELENTED AND AGREED TO NEEDLE HOMELESS BRENDA..
BUT THE DAMAGE HAD BEEN DONE..ONE TIME STACY FANS HAD FORMED THE LI'L ADAM HABIT AND WERE LOST TO ME FOREVER..
PLEASE READ NICK STACY SOMEBODY PLEASE
The BUGLE
IN CENTRAL CITY NEARLY EVERYONE READS FEARFUL FOOZNIK
THE COURIER

AND SO YOU WENT THERE TONIGHT AND KILLED HIM?
YES, HA HA... I SHOT HIM AS HE LAY SLEEPING OVER HIS BOARD.. HA HA I'M GLAD, GLAD DO YOU HEAR... STAND BACK.. YOU WON'T TAKE ME ALIVE!
MEANWHILE..
SLAPP IS OUT OF HIS COMA..
WELL HEH HEH.. THINK I'LL GO NOW..
NO, YOU WONT! BOOK THIS MAN FOR ATTEMPTED MURDER, DOLAN... GHOUL WAS INNOCENT... MATRIX STABBED SLAPP!
BUT WHAT'S HIS MOTIVE?
YAWWN.. OW! I'VE A CRICK IN MY NECK... OH, HELLO, MATRIX. YAWWN.. NO USE THREATENING... I'M LEAVING YOUR SYNDICATE TO SIGN WITH RICHARD HEADLINE SMIRCH!
THERE'S THE MOTIVE... SLAPP IS THE BEST MAN THEY HAVE... THE BIG SOURCE OF THEIR INCOME!
OOPS... EXCUSE ME... I'VE A DEADLINE TO MEET... I'LL SEND YOU ALL AN ORIGINAL SOME TIME!
SLAM
POW
AAAH!!
GO AHEAD.. ARREST ME FO' ASSAULT 'N' BATTERY.. FO' Y'ARS THET VARMINT'S BEEN MAKIN' FUN O' US HILL FOLK.. AH'M GITTEN MAHTY PEEKID AT HIM MAKIN' US OUT STUPID... AT LAST AH CAUGHT UP WIF HIM!

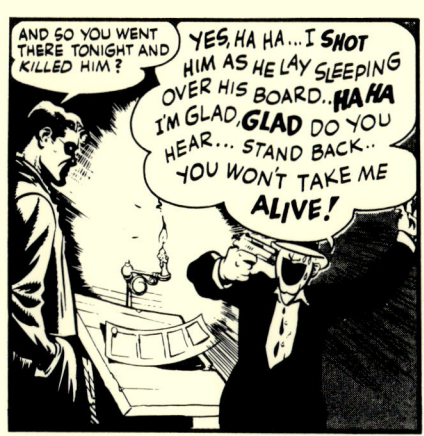

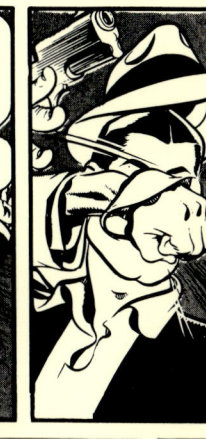

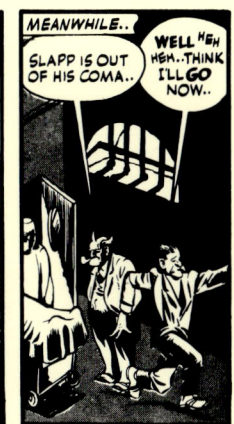

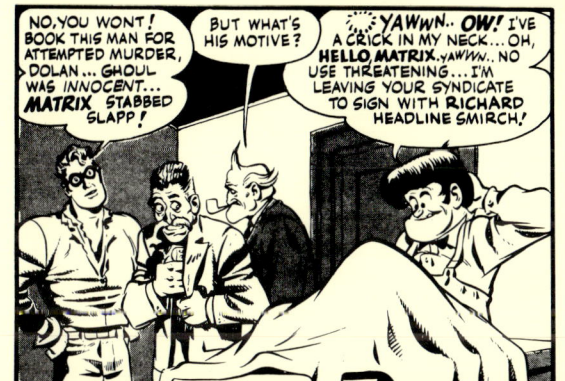

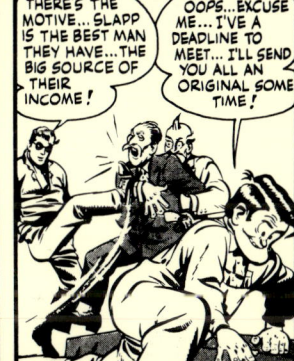

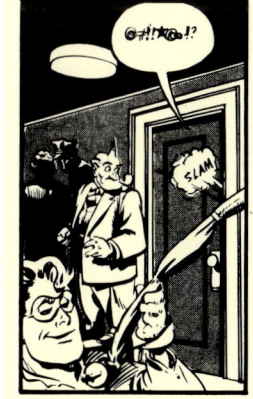

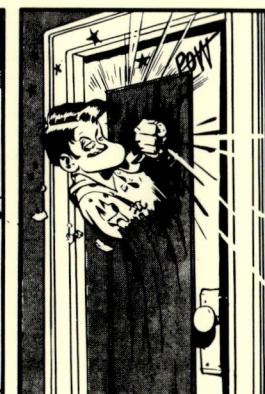

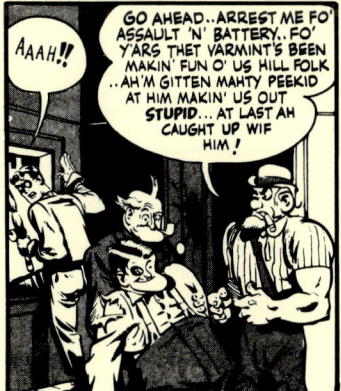

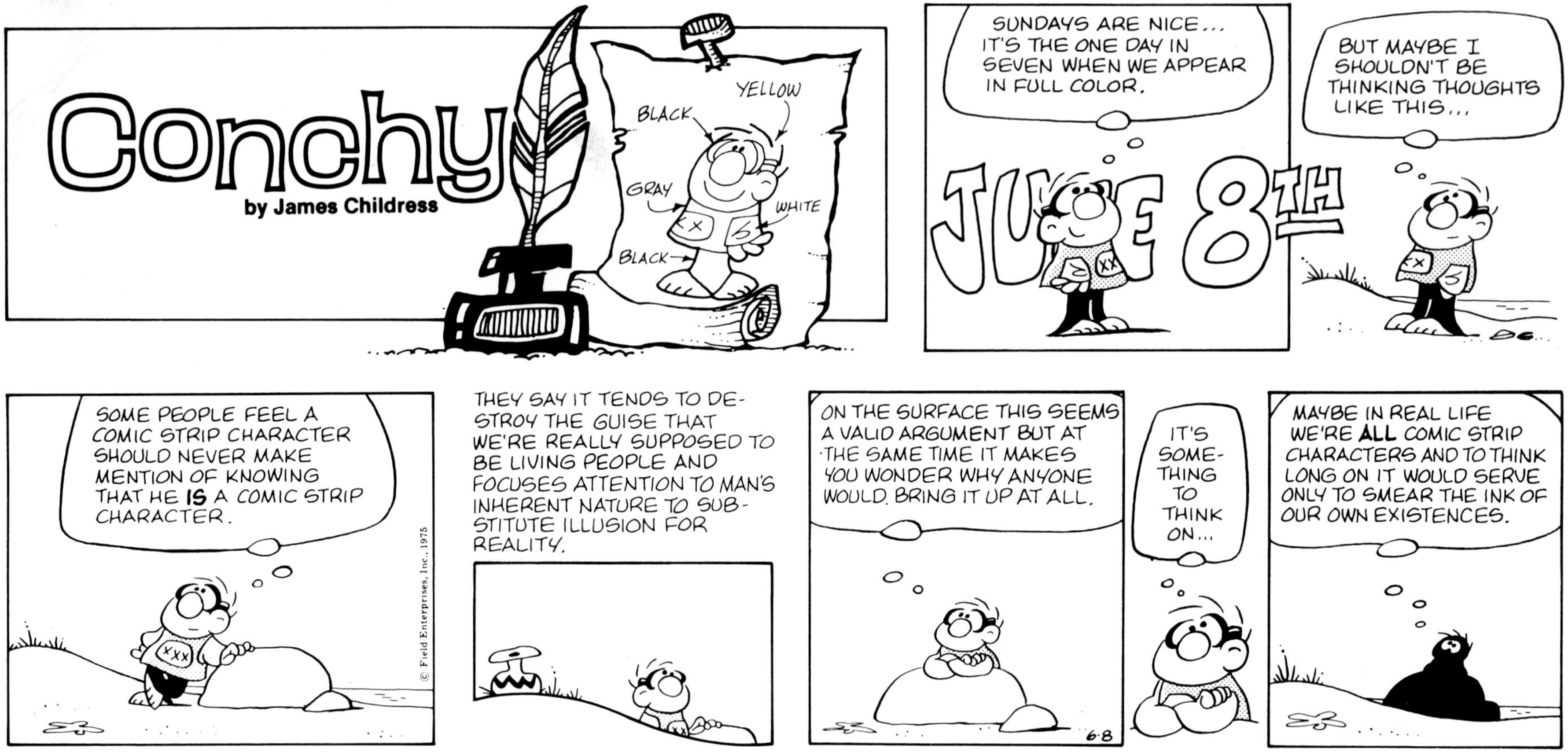
Conchy
by James Childress
YELLOW
BLACK
GRAY
WHITE
BLACK
SUNDAYS ARE NICE... IT'S THE ONE DAY IN SEVEN WHEN WE APPEAR IN FULL COLOR.
JUNE 8TH
BUT MAYBE I SHOULDN'T BE THINKING THOUGHTS LIKE THIS...
SOME PEOPLE FEEL A COMIC STRIP CHARACTER SHOULD NEVER MAKE MENTION OF KNOWING THAT HE IS A COMIC STRIP CHARACTER.
© Field Enterprises, Inc., 1975
THEY SAY IT TENDS TO DESTROY THE GUISE THAT WE'RE REALLY SUPPOSED TO BE LIVING PEOPLE AND FOCUSES ATTENTION TO MAN'S INHERENT NATURE TO SUBSTITUTE ILLUSION FOR REALITY.
ON THE SURFACE THIS SEEMS A VALID ARGUMENT BUT AT THE SAME TIME IT MAKES YOU WONDER WHY ANYONE WOULD BRING IT UP AT ALL.
6·8
IT'S SOMETHING TO THINK ON...
MAYBE IN REAL LIFE WE'RE ALL COMIC STRIP CHARACTERS AND TO THINK LONG ON IT WOULD SERVE ONLY TO SMEAR THE INK OF OUR OWN EXISTENCES.

James Childress *Conchy*
8 June 1975.
Reprinted by special permission of King Features Syndicate.